The Internet Under Crisis Conditions
Learning from September 11

Committee on the Internet Under Crisis Conditions:
Learning from September 11

Computer Science and Telecommunications Board
Division on Engineering and Physical Sciences

NATIONAL RESEARCH COUNCIL
OF THE NATIONAL ACADEMIES

THE NATIONAL ACADEMIES PRESS
Washington, D.C.
www.nap.edu

THE NATIONAL ACADEMIES PRESS   500 Fifth Street, N.W.   Washington, DC 20001

NOTICE: The project that is the subject of this report was approved by the Governing Board of the National Research Council, whose members are drawn from the councils of the National Academy of Sciences, the National Academy of Engineering, and the Institute of Medicine. The members of the committee responsible for the report were chosen for their special competences and with regard for appropriate balance.

Support for this project was provided by the Association for Computing Machinery's Special Interest Group in Data Communication (ACM SIGCOMM); the IBM Corporation; and the Vadasz Family Foundation, a contributor to the Computer Science and Telecommunications Board's program on information technology and society. Any opinions, findings, conclusions, or recommendations expressed in this publication are those of the authors and do not necessarily reflect the views of the organizations that provided support for the project.

International Standard Book Number 0-309-08702-3

Cover image courtesy of Verizon Communications. Cover designed by Jennifer Bishop.

Copies of this report are available from the National Academies Press, 500 Fifth Street, N.W., Lockbox 285, Washington, DC 20055; (800) 624-6242 or (202) 334-3313 in the Washington metropolitan area. Internet, http://www.nap.edu.

THE NATIONAL ACADEMIES
Advisers to the Nation on Science, Engineering, and Medicine

The **National Academy of Sciences** is a private, nonprofit, self-perpetuating society of distinguished scholars engaged in scientific and engineering research, dedicated to the furtherance of science and technology and to their use for the general welfare. Upon the authority of the charter granted to it by the Congress in 1863, the Academy has a mandate that requires it to advise the federal government on scientific and technical matters. Dr. Bruce M. Alberts is president of the National Academy of Sciences.

The **National Academy of Engineering** was established in 1964, under the charter of the National Academy of Sciences, as a parallel organization of outstanding engineers. It is autonomous in its administration and in the selection of its members, sharing with the National Academy of Sciences the responsibility for advising the federal government. The National Academy of Engineering also sponsors engineering programs aimed at meeting national needs, encourages education and research, and recognizes the superior achievements of engineers. Dr. Wm. A. Wulf is president of the National Academy of Engineering.

The **Institute of Medicine** was established in 1970 by the National Academy of Sciences to secure the services of eminent members of appropriate professions in the examination of policy matters pertaining to the health of the public. The Institute acts under the responsibility given to the National Academy of Sciences by its congressional charter to be an adviser to the federal government and, upon its own initiative, to identify issues of medical care, research, and education. Dr. Harvey V. Fineberg is president of the Institute of Medicine.

The **National Research Council** was organized by the National Academy of Sciences in 1916 to associate the broad community of science and technology with the Academy's purposes of furthering knowledge and advising the federal government. Functioning in accordance with general policies determined by the Academy, the Council has become the principal operating agency of both the National Academy of Sciences and the National Academy of Engineering in providing services to the government, the public, and the scientific and engineering communities. The Council is administered jointly by both Academies and the Institute of Medicine. Dr. Bruce M. Alberts and Dr. Wm. A. Wulf are chair and vice chair, respectively, of the National Research Council.

www.national-academies.org

JANICE SABUDA, Senior Project Assistant
JENNIFER BISHOP, Senior Project Assistant
BRANDYE WILLIAMS, Office Assistant

Preface

Although secondary to the human tragedy resulting from the September 11, 2001, attacks on the World Trade Center and the Pentagon, telecommunications issues were significant that day both in terms of damage (physical as well as functional) and of mounting response and recovery efforts. The Internet has come to be a major component of the nation's (and the world's) communications and information infrastructure. People rely on it for business, social, and personal activities of many kinds, and government depends on it for communications and transactions with the media and the public. Thus there is interest in how the Internet performed and was used on September 11.

Unlike the situation with longer-standing telecommunications services (notably the public telephone network), there are few regulations, policies, or practices related to the Internet's functioning in emergency situations. Nor are there many publicly available data to help policy makers or the industry itself assess the Internet's performance—either on a continuing basis or in the aftermath of a crisis. No regular system exists for reporting failures and outages, nor is there agreement on metrics of performance.[1] Some experiences are shared informally among network

---

[1] A pilot effort was made by the Federal Communications Commission to collect outage information under the auspices of the Network Reliability and Interoperability Council, but this was limited to a voluntary trial, recently ended in 2002. Interest in mounting a new voluntary effort continues in some quarters.

operators or in forums such as the North American Network Operators Group (NANOG), but that information is not readily accessible for national planning or research purposes. The decentralized architecture of the Internet—although widely characterized as one of the Internet's strengths—further confounds the difficulty of collecting comprehensive data about how the Internet is performing.

It is therefore unsurprising that no definitive analyses exist on the impact of September 11 on the Internet, though a few conflicting anecdotal reports about its performance that day—such as several presentations at NANOG indicating relatively little effect[2] and press accounts suggesting that the impact was severe[3]—have appeared.

Responding to an initial request in early 2002 from the Association for Computing Machinery's Special Interest Group in Data Communication (ACM SIGCOMM), the Computer Science and Telecommunications Board (CSTB) established the Committee on the Internet Under Crisis Conditions: Learning from the Impact of September 11. The committee's charge was twofold: to organize an exploratory workshop for gathering data and accounts of experiences pertinent to the impact of September 11 on the Internet, and to prepare a report that summarizes the Internet's performance that day and offers conclusions on better preparing for and responding to future emergencies.

A diverse group of industry representatives and researchers participated in the workshop (see Appendix A). They were invited to share information candidly, with the understanding that the organizing committee would take care not to publish sensitive or proprietary information. Consequently, although the committee has strived to present as much detail as possible, specific figures or names of organizations have been omitted in some instances. Following the workshop, the study committee decided to supplement what was obtained there, so additional information in several areas was gathered from a number of sources.

---

[2]North American Network Operators Group 23rd Meeting, October 21-23, 2001, Oakland, Calif. Presentations available online at <http://www.nanog.org/mtg-0110/agenda.html>.

[3]According to an article in *ComputerWorld*: "Extent of cyberinfrastructure devastation on Sept. 11 unprecedented, officials say. For several tense hours on Sept. 11, the nation was deaf, dumb and blind due to the 'absolutely massive' loss of communications infrastructure resulting from the collapse of the World Trade Center, a senior government official said last week." The article goes on to focus on consequences of damage to a Verizon central office but implies much wider impact. Dan Verton. 2002. "Digital Destruction Was Worst Imaginable," *ComputerWorld*, March 4. Available online at <http://www.computerworld.com/managementtopics/management/recovery/story/0,10801,68762,00.html>.

The overall human and economic costs of the September 11 attacks—which dwarf in significance the attacks' effects on the Internet—have been widely covered and are not examined here. Instead, this report focuses on three issues related to the Internet: (1) the local, national, and global consequences of the destruction that occurred in New York City; (2) the impact of the crisis, including the actions of users as well as the effects of the physical damage; and (3) how people made use of the Internet in a time of crisis.

The project was small—reflecting its relatively narrow focus and the objective of producing a report quickly—and had limited resources. These considerations, combined with the relative paucity of data, mean that the committee's assessment was not comprehensive. Instead, the committee examined several sources of data that revealed the overall status of the Internet on September 11 as well as shortly thereafter, and it drew on the detailed experiences of several Internet service providers. This was sufficient to derive a rough sense of that day's impact on the Internet infrastructure nationwide—and worldwide.

The committee and the CSTB acknowledge the financial support provided for this project by ACM SIGCOMM, the IBM Corporation, and the Vadasz Family Foundation. Their support enabled but did not influence the outcome of the committee's work.

The committee also wishes to thank the workshop participants for their thoughtful contributions and for their comments on a draft of this report. Responsibility for the report, however, remains with the authoring committee.

Acknowledgment of Reviewers

This report has been reviewed in draft form by individuals chosen for their diverse perspectives and technical expertise, in accordance with procedures approved by the National Research Council's Report Review Committee. The purpose of this independent review is to provide candid and critical comments that will assist the institution in making its published report as sound as possible and to ensure that the report meets institutional standards for objectivity, evidence, and responsiveness to the study charge. The review comments and draft manuscript remain confidential to protect the integrity of the deliberative process. We wish to thank the following individuals for their review of this report:

Geoffrey Baehr, U.S. Venture Partners,
Steven Bellovin, AT&T Labs—Research,
Scott Bradner, Harvard University,
Geraldine MacDonald, America Online, Inc.,
Udi Manber, Yahoo! Inc., and
Andrew Odlyzko, University of Minnesota.

Although the reviewers listed above provided many constructive comments and suggestions, they were not asked to endorse the conclusions or recommendations, nor did they see the final draft of the report before its release. The review of this report was overseen by Robert R. Everett, Honorary Trustee of the MITRE Corporation. Appointed by the National Research Council, he was responsible for making certain that an independent examination of this report was carried out in accordance with institutional procedures and that all review comments were carefully considered. Responsibility for the final content of this report rests entirely with the authoring committee and the institution.

Contents

Summary and Findings

OVERVIEW

The events of September 11, 2001, in addition to their other consequences, caused localized physical damage to the Internet in one of the network's most important hubs, New York City. Communications infrastructure located in the World Trade Center itself and nearby at the Verizon central office at 140 West Street, along with fiber-optic cables that ran under the Trade Center complex, was destroyed. Electrical power in Lower Manhattan was disrupted, and local telecommunications facilities there suffered a variety of problems with their backup power systems.

Serious effects on communications networks, however, were confined to New York City and a few other regions highly dependent on it for their connectivity. In some cases, automatic rerouting at the physical or network levels allowed Internet traffic to bypass many of the infrastructure's failed parts. Most local Internet-connectivity problems that could not be resolved by automatic rerouting were fixed within hours or days through the rapid deployment of new equipment or reconfiguration of the system.

Although users outside New York City were also affected by the events of September 11, most of the difficulties experienced were not due to serious problems in the Internet infrastructure itself but rather to disruptions stemming from subtle interdependencies between systems—it turned out that some services depended indirectly on connections made in New York City.

Even though their network connectivity had not been impaired, many users had difficulty reading some popular news Web sites. Unprecedented levels of user demand immediately following the attack severely stressed the server computers for these sites. Web service providers quickly took a number of steps—such as reducing the complexity of Web pages, using alternative mechanisms for distributing content, and reallocating computing resources—to respond successfully to demand.

Despite these problems, the Internet, taken as a whole, was not significantly affected. For example, it did not suffer the kinds of overloads that are often associated with the telephone system in a time of crisis. The resilience of the network during the September 11 crisis was a credit to the ingenuity and perseverance of the people who worked to restore communication service near the attack sites; and fundamentally, it was testimony to the Internet's inherently flexible and robust design.

However, the Internet's performance on September 11 does not necessarily indicate how it might respond to being directly targeted. Furthermore, it is clear that the experience of individual Internet service providers (ISPs) and corporate networks on September 11 does not generalize: damage suffered, and ability to respond, varied widely from place to place. In particular, the modest effect on Internet communications overall does not indicate how well an individual ISP (and its customers) would fare in an attack targeted specifically to that ISP. Representatives of several ISPs told the committee that what made September 11 a relatively untroubled (albeit unnerving) day for them was simply the fact that their facilities were not concentrated at 140 West Street. But the experience did establish the Internet's *overall* resilience in the face of significant infrastructural damage.

FINDINGS

The workshop organized by the Committee on the Internet Under Crisis Conditions: Learning from the Impact of September 11 yielded a number of insights about what happened and did not happen to the Internet as a result of the attacks of September 11, 2001. It also provided a number of lessons learned that could reduce the impact of future crises, and it pointed to some ways in which the Internet itself could play a greater role in crisis response.

Finding 1. The events of September 11 had little effect on Internet services as a whole. The network displayed considerable flexibility that underscored its adaptability in the face of infrastructure damage and the demands imposed by a crisis.

In much of the data that the committee examined, an observer would be hard-pressed to find any unusual impact from the events of September

11 outside the immediately affected areas. Connectivity indeed dropped on the morning of September 11 at some locations in the Internet, and it dropped as well during several subsequent intervals when electrical-power disruptions affected telecommunications facilities in Lower Manhattan. But connectivity recovered quickly, and the magnitude of its loss was actually less than has been seen in other incidents affecting the Internet. For some users, however, the events of September 11 significantly affected their Internet experience, disrupting their connectivity altogether or limiting their ability to obtain information from certain news sites.

Measures of overall Internet traffic suggest that traffic volumes were somewhat lower on September 11 than on a typical business day, with many who normally would have been using the Internet turning to television for news and to phone calls for reaching loved ones. Traffic did increase in two areas—the quest for news and the use of Internet communications as a substitute for telephone calls. News Web sites, straining under unprecedented levels of demand, took a number of steps to enhance their ability to handle the traffic (Box 3.1 in Chapter 3 describes CNN's experience in particular and the strategies it employed). Low-bandwidth e-mail and instant messaging were used as substitutes for telephone service, especially where conventional-telephone and cellular network congestion was high.

Overall, the Internet experience on September 11 was in no way comparable to the trials of some other communications media, such as the cellular phone services in greater New York, which suffered from local infrastructure damage and regional congestion. In part, this difference reflects the Internet's unique design (described in Box 4.1 in Chapter 4).

A number of examples of how the Internet was used in the hours and days immediately following the September 11 attacks highlight the flexibility afforded by that design. NYSERNet, a nonprofit networking consortium, was able to reroute connectivity to bypass physical damage in Lower Manhattan. It proved relatively easy to reconnect the New York Academy of Medicine to the Internet by means of a jury-rigged wireless link. When telephone service was impaired (through local damage to telephone circuits and disruption of some toll-free systems), some network operators were able to use instant messaging and voice-over-Internet Protocol (IP) to coordinate activities. CNN and other information providers adapted their content and modified the ways in which they delivered Web data to accommodate the extraordinary demand for news. A wireless instant-messaging service saw increased use on September 11 and in the following days. Various groups rapidly set up Web sites for exchanging information on the disaster and the possible whereabouts of missing people.

An important point about these responses is that they required no central coordination. Individuals and groups were able to spontaneously craft solutions to their problems and to deploy them quickly.

Finding 2. While the committee is confident in its assessment that the events of September 11 had little effect on the Internet as a whole (Finding 1), the precision with which analysts can measure the impact of such events is limited by a lack of relevant data.

The data available to the committee to gauge the impact of September 11 included active measurements of packet delay and loss over a small fraction of the Internet's paths, selected passive monitoring of application-level behavior and global-routing activity, and data from a survey of Internet users. In some cases, this information was sufficient for drawing qualitative conclusions. But the committee's examination also revealed the paucity of Internet data available to the research community. Available data are limited for reasons that include the following:

- *Factors intrinsic to the Internet's design.* One cannot, for example, determine how many individual users are actually affected by the loss of routes to a particular set of addresses. It is also hard to know if users who have lost connectivity through one route have reestablished connectivity through another one—new connections might have been made at a higher level of aggregation, in which case data showing fewer routes available would not mean worse connectivity.
- *Modest size of the measurement universe.* The measurements of Internet activity that are made on a regular basis are rather limited. For example, connectivity is monitored to some extent by examining routing tables, but only from particular vantage points. Routes themselves are periodically traced to probe connectivity, but only with coarse time granularity. Data collected on traffic volumes (workload) are often considered proprietary, and much of the measurement of Internet activities is conducted by small research groups with modest resources. Moreover, the available analysis and modeling tools for probing Internet behavior could be much improved.
- *Tendency to simply discard data.* Even when information is collected, it is often retained only for a short time. In a number of cases, requests for workload data and other detailed logs of Internet activity during September 11 showed that the data had already been discarded by the time of the committee's March 2002 workshop.
- *Nonavailability of good measures of the overall state of the Internet.* One of the consequences of the fragmented and often proprietary measurement infrastructure is that data are gathered piecemeal in diverse ways and stored in various formats; there is no commonly accepted way of

standardizing what information is collected and integrating the data to enable characterization of the Internet's overall health. Therefore, ready comparison of September 11 to a "typical" day was not possible. The information available to the committee generally permitted only rough comparisons in the context of a particular set of data (e.g., data on the reachability of a particular set of Internet addresses suggest that the effects of September 11 were similar to those of a severed fiber-optic cable). One exception was that some conclusions could be drawn about the Internet as a whole when specific measurements could be correlated with data from surveys of Internet users (which are designed to be representative of all U.S. users).

The inability to measure in detail the effects of September 11 on the Internet does not by itself provide a clear mandate for building a new and widespread Internet measurement system, which would be both complex and costly. Gathering data across all Internet providers would probably require new regulations to compel their cooperation. There is, however, a relatively easy way to help improve understanding of the Internet's behavior during crises or other anomalous events: simply holding on to the relevant data. One lesson from September 11 with regard to Internet measurement is that important data from such circumstances are typically discarded soon after the fact. It may be useful to find ways to alert network managers to the importance of archiving data collected during significant events so that more detailed analysis can be performed later on.

Finding 3. The events of September 11 did have a major effect on the services offered by some information and service providers.

Although the Internet as a whole was largely unaffected by the events of September 11, those services and service providers that *were* affected were often hit hard. The surge in demand for news overwhelmed the Web-server capacity of at least two major news services, for example, and nearby infrastructure serving the New York Stock Exchange and its member firms was heavily damaged.

Also, while many of the effects of September 11 were highly localized (like the attacks themselves), some parties far from the physical disaster sites were affected—ISPs in parts of Europe lost connectivity because they interconnected with the rest of the Internet in New York City, and South Africa experienced disruptions associated with the Domain Name System (DNS).

Finding 4. People's use of Internet services on and immediately following September 11 differed from what has been typical.

People used the Internet very differently in the aftermath of the September 11 attacks. For example, they sent less e-mail overall (although some substituted e-mail for phoning where the telephone networks were congested), and they used news sites more heavily. They made greater use of instant messaging. The overall picture that emerges is that individuals used the Internet to supplement the information received from television (which was the preferred source of news). Those unable to view television often substituted Internet news. The telephone, meanwhile, remained the preferred means of communicating with friends and loved ones, but chat rooms and e-mail were also used, especially where the telephone infrastructure was damaged or overloaded.

The levels of other activities on the Internet, such as e-commerce, declined. One consequence of this decrease was that in spite of larger numbers of person-to-person communications, total load on the Internet decreased rather than increased, so that the network was not at risk of congestion.

Finding 5. September 11 demonstrated the Internet's overall resilience to physical attacks. But it also revealed that in parts of the system, redundancy appears to have been inadequate.

The attacks of September 11 were not directed at the Internet. Nonetheless, because New York City is a major worldwide data-communications hub and a number of key communications links and facilities were concentrated in a handful of sites near the World Trade Center complex, the attack caused significant damage to Internet elements. On the basis of its analyses of the effects of the attack, of steps taken to restore connectivity, and of various "what if" scenarios, the committee concludes that the richness of the Internet's interconnectivity provides effective protection against a localized physical attack. Although the committee heard from workshop participants that a carefully designed, distributed attack against a number of physical locations, especially if carried out in a repeating pattern, could be highly disruptive, it concluded that an attack at a single point or a small number of points is probably survivable.

Regarding the infrastructural damage that occurred on September 11, the level of Internet redundancy was adequate outside the immediately affected area. However, parts of the Internet were not as redundant as one might suppose. Links that were logically distinct turned out to run over the same fiber spans or to be connected to major systems through the same trenches or buildings. Co-location of capacity and equipment cuts expenses, but it obviously increases vulnerability to common outages. Improving the robustness of the communications infrastructure may require conscious trade-offs between reliability and cost. Finally, certain providers and certain regions of the world are heavily dependent on a few key connection points; diversifying those points would significantly improve robustness.

The connectivity problems outside New York City illustrate that end-to-end communication on the Internet depends on the functioning of several different (often geographically separate) systems such as local phone lines, modem banks, authentication servers, and DNS servers. In addition, some wireless applications (handheld devices at hospitals, for example) depend on Internet access to reach application services located in the same building. A hospital in New York City learned on September 11 that wireless personal digital assistants (PDAs), on which doctors rely to access medical information, were connected through an external ISP network. Thus when the hospital's sole link to the Internet was briefly broken by the collapse of the Twin Towers, doctors had trouble accessing hospital records. ISPs and users alike should be aware of these potential vulnerabilities and take appropriate steps to improve redundancy where connectivity is mission-critical.

Finding 6. The Internet experience on September 11 exposed a number of subtle operational issues that merit attention from users and operators.

Most disasters impart useful lessons on what might be done better in the future. The September 11 experiences of ISPs and users were no exception:

- *Internet operations depend on the public telephone network.* One specific vulnerability is the use of toll-free telephone numbers for communicating between different ISP operation centers. This practice makes Internet operations vulnerable to outages in the toll-free system (which involves an extra database lookup as compared with direct-dialing of a toll call). And the toll-free system indeed had a partial failure on September 11 as a result of call volume, complicating ISP coordination. More generally, although the public telephone network and the Internet are for the most part logically distinct, they are closely tied physically because both depend on the same fiber-optic infrastructure. This shared vulnerability suggests that in the future the two networks be analyzed together; for example, to what degree are they dependent on the same physical facilities and to what degree can they actually substitute for one another?
- *Telecommunications-facility disaster planning should factor in support for operational personnel, and ensuring a capability for remote operation should be considered wherever possible.* One ISP reported difficulty in feeding its operations staff, as all the businesses around its center in Northern Virginia had closed. There was some difficulty getting diesel fuel delivered to backup power generators serving telecommunications facilities in

Lower Manhattan. Key data centers were sometimes inaccessible as a result of areawide closures, even though they themselves had not suffered damage. Operators that could manage their sites remotely, however, reported that this capability was valuable for keeping services running.

• *Key businesses and services that must operate in a disaster should examine their dependence on Internet connections and plan accordingly.* Several examples of interdependencies arose in workshop discussions: (1) a New York City hospital relied on an external Internet link to connect wireless PDAs, (2) the NYC.gov Web site was disconnected from the Internet by the attack, and (3) major news sites had difficulty accommodating higher demand. Specific responses that may be appropriate for organizations and Web sites likely to be used in an emergency include these: (1) providing redundant network connectivity (from more than one network provider and by way of more than one physical link or conduit), (2) performing an end-to-end audit of Internet dependencies, and (3) establishing plans for dealing with greatly increased traffic loads.

• *Network operators and telecommunications interconnection facility operators should review their emergency power procedures.* Power problems caused transient disruptions to Internet connectivity as well as possible damage to the equipment because of overheating (when cooling systems failed). Most network operators and ISPs had already established procedures for dealing with power failures, and in New York City these procedures generally worked as planned. But not enough attention appears to have been paid to the possibility that some backup systems could fail. For example, a number of disruptions to the Internet occurred 8 to 12 hours after the power was shut off in Lower Manhattan because backup batteries and generators failed. Reports also suggest that ISPs, unlike some other utilities, were not granted access to the restricted zone in Lower Manhattan, which further complicated their recovery efforts. Specific problems included these:

—Poor operating procedure resulted in a facility's backup generator being shut off to conserve fuel, which in turn led to service interruptions when grid electrical power was lost.

—Fuel delivery problems, including delivery of the wrong type of fuel to one location, made it difficult to keep generators running.

—Communications equipment was allowed to continue operating even when electrical power necessary for cooling systems had been lost.

—Fiber termination circuits were not connected to generators and failed when their 8-hour batteries failed.

—Backup generators shut down when their air intake filters became clogged with dust, a problem that could possibly have been averted if more rapid access for maintenance had been possible.

Several prudent steps could be taken to reduce future disruptions. Operators should evaluate their vulnerabilities to multiday electrical outages. In particular, the evaluation should determine the primary and backup power source for every major device (server, router, switch) and independently powered link (e.g., Synchronous Optical Network [SONET] or point-to-point fiber). Operators should also identify how each device will respond to a power outage (after both primary and backup power fail) and how it will resume functioning when power is restored. Operators should develop contingency plans that allow them to provide services for the maximum period of time (in particular, all key devices should use the longest-lived backup power supplies available) and restore most services remotely after an outage. Operators should also identify special needs (e.g., fuel for generators and the space in which to place additional generators if they are needed) that may require the consent of local authorities, and they should have plans for coordinating with authorities in the event of an emergency.

Finding 7. The experience gained from the events of September 11 points to ways in which the Internet could be better leveraged in future crises.

It is reasonable to anticipate—and thus to plan for—increased use of the Internet in future crises, and lessons learned from September 11 indicate some of the issues that deserve attention.

On the one hand, it is clear that in the immediate aftermath of a disaster, people will typically turn on television sets (to get news) and call family and friends on the telephone (to convey news, report on their status, or supplement television news with information of a more personal nature); they tend not to use the Internet. The data from September 11 show that this pattern held on that day; even heavy Internet users went first to the television and the telephone.

On the other hand, it is also clear that if the television or telephone was unavailable or failed to provide the information people needed, they turned to the Internet even if they normally were not heavy Internet users. For instance, it appears that much of the surge in demand at online news sites on the morning of September 11 came from people who did not have access to television sets at their workplace. People also appear to have used the Internet to supplement information available from other sources, as evidenced by marked shifts in topics searched on the Internet. These behaviors suggest that disaster planning should include examination of how the Internet might be used to disseminate information in a future crisis.

The experiences of September 11 also indicate the value of efficient Internet or Internet-style data communication in a disaster. These alternatives, such as text messaging and e-mail, make more efficient use of limited communications capacity than do other services. By midday on September 11, the cellular-phone networks in Manhattan were severely congested, yet there are reports that people who used their cell phones or wireless-equipped PDAs to send instant messages were able to communicate effectively. E-mail and instant messages were also used as a substitute for telephone calls.

Although better communication over the Internet could simply have been the result of the relative overprovisioning of the Internet-related communication infrastructure, there are several fundamental reasons why, for example, using a PDA to send a short text message such as "I'm OK and am walking home" is far more efficient and more likely to succeed than making a cell-phone call when the network is congested. First, the Internet degrades under load more gracefully than does the voice network. If sufficient capacity is not available, the cell-phone network will not permit new calls to be set up. In contrast, the Internet makes use of mechanisms that continue to accept new messages but reduce transmission rates when the network is congested. Also, by virtue of their flexible design, Internet-style communications lend themselves to human actions that reduce the load—whether by substituting a brief text message for a data-intensive voice call or removing data-intensive graphics from a Web page (as CNN did in the face of high loads). A lesson here is that organizations responsible for disaster planning should encourage awareness of this more efficient way to communicate.

1

Introduction

A BRIEF OVERVIEW OF THE INTERNET

The Internet is a worldwide collection of networks, operated by some 10,000 Internet service providers (ISPs),[1] that accommodates a diversity of applications such as e-mail, instant messaging, the World Wide Web, and numerous other, more specialized functions.

This system involves multinational telecommunications carriers, cable companies, corporate networks, nonprofit-organization networks, government-agency networks, sole proprietorships, and even hobbyists. Each network consists of a set of optical-fiber, copper-circuit, or wireless communications links that connect to "end-hosts"—desktop personal computers (PCs) or servers that provide Web content—or to specialized computers known as routers that control the paths taken by data packets. The interconnection of these networks is facilitated by a set of standardized protocols that determine how data and routing information are exchanged.

The networks of the Internet are not only interconnected but for the most part are *richly* interconnected. Its architecture, which dynamically adjusts the routes that packets follow in response to changes in the network (such as failures of communications links), emphasizes redun-

---

[1]*Boardwatch Magazine* (<http://www.boardwatch.com>) lists 9,400; CyberAtlas (<http://cyberatlas.internet.com/big_picture/geographics/article/0,,5911_151151,00.html>) puts the worldwide figure at more than 11,400.

dancy.[2] However, this redundancy has its limits; only a finite number of paths connect any given point to the rest of the system. Also, geography and economics mean that some locations have a high concentration of Internet facilities while others only have few.

New York City, a principal focus of this report, can be thought of as a "superconnected node." This is largely because the city has a great many Internet users, private data networks, ISPs, and fiber-optic grids.[3] For example, more than 600 dial-up ISPs and over 300 digital subscriber line (DSL) providers are listed in the ISP directory *Boardwatch* for the borough of Manhattan alone. Fiber-optic cables enter and exit Manhattan by way of at least five different rights-of-way. At least 74 U.S. and multinational telecommunications carriers have equipment in New York, either in co-location facilities or in private suites. The city is served by more than 100 international Internet carriers, and it has direct links with 71 countries.[4]

Connected to the Internet through the long-haul fiber networks of several major carriers, New York City is also a major interconnection point for these carriers.[5] Interconnection is for the most part done at one of several key "carrier hotels"—buildings in which carriers lease space in order to link with other carriers located in the same building. Internet providers connect with each other through private connections at the carrier hotels, either directly through Internet exchange points such as the New York Internet Exchange (NYIX) or indirectly through transit providers. Most transatlantic telecommunication cables landing along the New Jersey/New York coastline are "backhauled" to one of the Manhattan

---

[2]The redundancy and distributed character of the Internet clearly echo the design contemplated in Paul Baran's seminal studies of packet networks at RAND. The series, together with brief commentary, is available online at <http://www.rand.org/publications/RM/baran.list.html>.

[3]The Lower Manhattan Telecommunications Users' Working Group (LMTUWG. August 2002. *Building a 21st Century Telecom Infrastructure: Lower Manhattan Telecommunications Users' Working Group Findings and Recommendations*) reports six physically distinct fiber networks in Lower Manhattan (AT&T, Con Edison Communications, MCI WorldCom, Metromedia Fiber Network, Time Warner, and Verizon). Information supplied to the committee by Anthony Townsend indicates more than 40 providers of fiber in Manhattan, not all of which are physically distinct (because of sharing and resale by providers).

[4]Telegeography, Inc. October 2001. *Telegeography 2002: Global Statistics and Commentary*. Washington, D.C. Executive summary available online at <http://www.telegeography.com/ products/books/pg/pdf/pg2002_exe_sum.pdf>.

[5]In addition to New York City, Washington, D.C., stands out on the East Coast of the United States as having a high concentration of Internet facilities. Several Internet service providers maintain network-control and data centers near Washington, D.C., and in Northern Virginia. Thus, in most ISP networks, the New York City-to-Washington, D.C., corridor contains the largest number of circuits.

carrier hotels to facilitate interconnection with other network operators. In some cases, the only route by which carriers can interconnect with the transatlantic cables is at one of the New York City carrier hotels.

Local Internet access may be provided through a number of different technologies, including dial-up, integrated services digital network (ISDN), DSL, T-1, cable modem, wireless, and SONET fiber. Many of these connections take place over the network of the local exchange carrier, Verizon, and the long-haul fiber networks connect to Verizon's central offices as well. Several ISPs that have registered as competitive local exchange carriers (CLECs) also have equipment in these central offices; collocated equipment there connects their networks to Verizon facilities that in turn connect the ISPs to their customers through DSL or ISDN. Finally, dial-up customers use the Verizon local network to place phone calls to modems operated by their ISPs. Other high-speed local data circuits are supplied by such companies as Time Warner Cable, Frontier, Cablevision/Lightpath, Metromedia Fiber Network, Inc. (MFN), AT&T Local Services, and WorldCom.

WHAT WOULD IT MEAN FOR THE INTERNET TO FAIL?

There are two principal types of failure that the Internet can incur:

1. *Parts of the network, such as interconnection points or communications links, are damaged or destroyed, and consequently the Internet stops functioning as expected.* There are two obvious manifestations of this kind of failure. First, the Internet could be damaged enough that it is partitioned—split into separate networks—so that a user might be able to reach some Web sites or send e-mail to some places but unable to communicate with others. Second, the Internet could remain fully interconnected but the damage might cause a reduction in capacity that impairs the network's operation in a material way. That is, when some links are damaged and new routes are constructed by the network to bypass the failed components, the backup paths are often of lower bandwidth. Thus there is less overall capacity, and increased network congestion is a likely outcome. A user might, for example, experience significantly greater Web-page loading times and be unable to view video clips.

2. *Changes in network use result in higher loads that cause parts of the network to be overwhelmed by traffic.* For example, increased network use in a particular geographical area could overload the aggregate capacity connecting that area to the rest of the Internet. Or, increased demand on a particular service, such as a Web site, might exceed the capacity of the links to that service or the capacity of the computers providing it.

Both types of failure—whether or not either of them occurred as a result of the September 11 attacks—are considered in this report.

A BRIEF OVERVIEW OF EVENTS ON SEPTEMBER 11, 2001

As the catastrophe at the World Trade Center unfolded, elements of the communications and power infrastructures were impaired, damaged, or destroyed. Box 1.1 provides a detailed outline of what transpired on and immediately after September 11. Local effects, such as damage to Verizon switching centers and last-mile facilities, had direct effects on Lower Manhattan—notably, the loss of telephone lines and damage to the cellular-phone system. At the same time, the infrastructural damage had effects that extended beyond the immediate area. Following is a summary of the key events and their effects on telecommunications, including the Internet:

- *8:45–10:00 A.M.* Towers are attacked and set afire. Interior World Trade Center (WTC) communication is disrupted. Increased volume congests local exchanges and wireless networks. Limited physical damage occurs to the surrounding local telephone networks.
- *10:00–11:00 A.M.* Towers collapse. Because the WTC was a significant wireless repeater site, some wireless connectivity is disrupted (Sprint PCS, Verizon, AT&T Wireless). Several ISPs' points of presence (POPs) in the complex—those of WorldCom, AT&T Local Service, and Verizon/ Genuity—are destroyed. Some data and private-line services to a diverse set of customers in New York City, Connecticut, Massachusetts, and even some European locations are disrupted.
- *11:00 A.M.–5:00 P.M.* Local power failures occur and some equipment is switched over to battery and/or generators. Fires burn in the WTC complex.
- *5:20–5:40 P.M.* WTC Building 7 collapses, destroying a Consolidated Edison electrical substation in the process. The collapse also breaches the 140 West Street Verizon central office building, causing damage to equipment and the flooding of basement power systems. The fires, collapse, and flooding knock out much of the telecommunications service in Lower Manhattan.

Although there were other significant events on September 11, 2001, this report mainly examines those in New York City. The crash of United Airlines Flight 93 in Somerset County, Pennsylvania, and that of American Airlines Flight 77 into the Pentagon did not appear to have any additional impact on the public Internet's infrastructure—though they were definitely a factor in shaping how people made use of the network. The

BOX 1.1
Detailed Time Line of the Events of September 11, 2001, and the Days Immediately Following

Date and Time	Event	Internet Effect
9/11/2001		
7:59–8:42 A.M.	American Airlines Flight 11, United Airlines Flight 175, United Airlines Flight 93, and American Airlines Flight 77 take off.	
8:40 A.M.	Federal Aviation Administration (FAA) notifies North American Aerospace Defense Command (NORAD) American Flight 11 hijacked.	
8:43 A.M.	FAA notifies NORAD American Flight 175 hijacked.	
8:46 A.M.	American Airlines Flight 11 crashes into North Tower (WTC 1) of World Trade Center.	
8:46 A.M.	Fighter Scramble Order: two F-15s dispatched from Otis Air National Guard Base in Falmouth, Mass. (airborne 8:52 A.M.).	
8:52 A.M.	Port Authority Trans-Hudson (PATH) train service ordered stopped.	
9:02 A.M.	United Flight 175 crashes into South Tower (WTC 2).	BBC, CNN, MSNBC, New York Times, Yahoo news, and other news Web sites become extremely unresponsive. Smaller local and regional news sites such as sfgate.com and nando.net still responsive.
9:12 A.M.	"Rescue" PATH train departs WTC station.	
9:17 A.M.	FAA shuts down all New York City airports.	
9:21 A.M.	All bridges and tunnels in New York City closed.	

continues

BOX 1.1   Continued

Date and Time	Event	Internet Effect
9:24 A.M.	FAA notifies NORAD American Flight 77 hijacked; line kept open; United Flight 93 reported hijacked during same call.	
9:24 A.M.	Fighter Scramble Order: two F-16s dispatched from Langley Air Force Base, Va. (airborne 9:30 A.M.).	
9:32 A.M.	New York Stock Exchange closed.	
9:37 A.M.	American Flight 77 crashes into Pentagon.	
9:39 A.M.		All New York City VHF stations, except CBS 2, off the air. Many radio stations also off the air.
9:40 A.M.	FAA orders nationwide air traffic halt.	
9:45 A.M.	Passenger on United Flight 93 makes cell-phone call.	
10:03 A.M.	United Airlines Flight 93 crashes in Somerset County, Pa.	
10:05 A.M.	WTC 2 (South Tower) collapses.	Verizon (South Tower), Genuity POPs in World Trade Center destroyed, AT&T Local Services POP in sub-basement operating on battery power.
10:10 A.M.	Portion of Pentagon collapses.	
10:28 A.M.	WTC 1 (North Tower) collapses.	
10:31 A.M.		Transatlantic circuit reported down after North Tower collapse.
10:32 A.M.		ISP operators report traffic volume decreasing slightly on networks.
11:02 A.M.	All New York City bridges opened for outbound traffic only.	

BOX 1.1 Continued

Date and Time	Event	Internet Effect
11:12 A.M.		Hundreds of DS-3 circuits reported down in New York City.
11:39 A.M.		CNN.com back up with very low graphics.
1:02 P.M.	New York City Mayor Giuliani orders evacuation of Manhattan south of Canal Street.	
1:16 P.M.		WorldCom SS7 long-distance switch experiences problems.
2:26 P.M.		AT&T reports its long-distance network is intact, but some equipment was damaged in its local New York service.
3:48 P.M.		CNN.com employs Akamai content server network to increase capacity.
3:48 P.M.		Covad reports service affected by fire in/near 140 West Street central office.
4:35 P.M.	Commercial power fails because of fire at World Trade Center Building 7 (built over Consolidated Edison substation); Con Edison reports area bordered by Dover Street on the north, the East River to the east, William Street to the west, and Wall Street to the south without commercial power.	25 Broadway, 32 Old Slip, 140 West Street on generator power.
5:20 P.M.	World Trade Center Building 7 collapses.	Verizon's 140 West Street central office walls breached by falling steel beams.

continues

BOX 1.1   Continued

Date and Time	*Event*	*Internet Effect*
7:17 P.M.	U.S. Attorney General Ashcroft announces FBI has set up Web site for tips about the attacks: <www.ifccfbi.gov>.	
7:33 P.M.	Verizon announces payphones in Lower Manhattan free for local calls.	
8:30 P.M.	President Bush addresses the nation.	
9:54 P.M.	Federal Emergency Management Agency notifies primary Emergency Alert System stations by e-mail to "make any and all preparations" if primary communication methods fail (estimated time).	
10:07 P.M.		ISP dial-access equipment overheating in 32 Old Slip. Reduction in inbound calls from New York City area.
10:26 P.M.		Generator stopped at 32 Old Slip; some carriers on battery.
10:36 P.M.		Verizon circuits at 60 Hudson Street reported down.
11:21 P.M.		NYC.gov (161.185.0.0/ 16) offline.
9/12/2001		
1:09 A.M.		Generator started at 32 Old Slip; Verizon circuits still down.
2:30 A.M.		Sprint reports that power fluctuations at a New York City switching facility disrupted Sprint voice, data, and wireless in southern Connecticut.
9:00 P.M.	Incorrect report of structural problems at 60 Hudson Street.	

BOX 1.1 Continued

Date and Time	Event	Internet Effect
10:22 P.M.		NYC.gov restored online. Fuel truck allowed into area to refuel 25 Broadway.
9/13/2001		
5:38 P.M.		25 Broadway generator failure; some equipment on battery. SAIX (South Africa Internet Exchange), NYIX (New York Internet Exchange), DANTE, Teleglobe, and many other providers affected.
9:28 P.M.		25 Broadway generator repaired.
9:47 P.M.		25 Broadway generator fails (again).
9/14/2001		
11:59 A.M.		Fiber cut south of Washington, D.C. (MFN).
8:26 P.M.		32 Old Slip power fails.
8:55 P.M.		32 Old Slip power restored.
11:10 P.M.		25 Broadway restored on Consolidated Edison-supplied generator.
9/15/2001		
1:28 P.M.		25 Broadway generator out of fuel; because of misjudged fuel consumption and fuel-truck travel time.
8:03 P.M.		25 Broadway generator refueled.

SOURCE: Compiled from various news reports and reports obtained by the committee from representatives of various Internet service providers.

destruction at the Pentagon certainly had some effect on military communications, but those are not considered in this report. However, as is discussed in Chapter 2, indirect impacts on Internet operations in the Washington, D.C., metropolitan area were felt as the normal course of business was disrupted.

2

The Network Experience

September 11, 2001, started out more or less routinely on the Internet. Early Tuesday morning is a common time for Internet service providers (ISPs) to schedule maintenance activities on their network, and on that particular Tuesday there were some instances of delay or packet loss between 2:00 A.M. and 5:00 A.M., when Verizon updated software on East Coast frame-relay switches and other ISPs made changes in their networks. But by 6:00 A.M. Eastern time, it appears that the Internet routing and traffic loads were normal for the start of a workday.

That normalcy would be shattered for the Internet, as for so many other operations, when American Airlines Flight 11 crashed into the World Trade Center's North Tower at 8:46 A.M. Within minutes, major online news sites were struggling to serve between 3 and 10 times their normal load as Internet users sought details. One news Web site estimated that traffic to its Web servers was doubling every 7 minutes, beginning around 8:50 A.M., until about 9:30 A.M.

By just after 9 A.M., when United Airlines Flight 175 crashed into the World Trade Center's South Tower, the Web sites of CNN, MSNBC, the New York Times, Yahoo! News, and others were observed to be slowing significantly. The cause would later be reported to have been the loads on these sites' servers, not connectivity problems in reaching servers across the Internet. Then the South Tower collapsed, damaging equipment and circuits in the Trade Center complex. The subsequent collapse of the North Tower, the collapse of World Trade Center Building 7 (a 47-story structure), damage to the neighboring Verizon central office, and power cuts in Lower Manhattan all had disruptive effects on the Internet and other communications systems.

How did the Internet's communications infrastructure in particular experience all these events? How much did the events in New York City, and in Washington, D.C., affect the movement of data throughout the Internet? How were ISPs affected by the events of September 11? How serious were the impacts? What actions did ISPs (and others) take in response?

This chapter sets out to answer those questions, as best they can be answered with the available information. Data pertaining to the Internet operations that day were of two types: quantitative data on the system as a whole and on the response of particular networks, and anecdotal reports from network operators, users, and news media that help provide context and possible explanations for the changes on the Internet, both at the macro and micro levels, that were deemed necessary after the attacks.

How comprehensive and authoritative is this information? Some of it—for example, data on changes in the Internet's routing configurations—permit the overall impact on the Internet to be measured. Reports on specific incidents, on the other hand, do not allow generalizations about the whole system, though they do provide insights into the kinds of local problems that could arise in the future and the responses that may mitigate them. Still, the participation in this study of several national ISPs and one New York regional ISP, together with the anecdotal information obtained though informal information-sharing relationships within the Internet operator community, permit at least a reasonable sampling of the overall experience. In addition, user surveys taken by the Pew Internet and American Life project allowed the committee to relate reported user behavior to some ISP measurements.[1] However, in a number of instances, data that would inform the committee's understanding of what transpired on and shortly after September 11 were lacking (a detailed discussion of Internet-measurement issues is presented in Chapter 5).

OVERVIEW OF DAMAGE AND IMPAIRMENT

The terrorist attacks in New York City caused an immediate disruption in communications within the World Trade Center complex. Soon thereafter, the collapse of the Twin Towers damaged and destroyed equipment of several wireless providers and some data circuits serving the

---

[1]Lee Raime and Bente Kalsnes. 2001. *The Commons of the Tragedy: How the Internet Was Used by Millions After the Terror Attacks to Grieve, Console, Share News, and Debate the Country's Response.* Pew Internet & American Life Project, Washington, D.C., October 10. Available online at <http://www.pewinternet.org/reports/toc.asp?Report=46>.

New York City area, the northeastern United States, and Europe. During the rest of the day on September 11, local power failures caused temporary equipment outages.

These events had several types of effects on ISPs and Internet users, including the following:

- *Loss of Internet connectivity in the vicinity of the attacks.* The effects in New York City were extensive as a result of the catastrophic damage at the World Trade Center site, the large number of nearby institutions, and the important role that New York City plays in the Internet infrastructure. Two main factors contributed to the loss of Internet connectivity—the permanent destruction of networking equipment at the site and the loss of power and cooling in adjacent areas for varying lengths of time. (By contrast, the attack in Washington, D.C., did not appear to have a direct influence on network connectivity for institutions outside the Pentagon.)

- *Connectivity loss at "out of town" locations in the United States and in other parts of the world.* Several ISPs elsewhere in the United States and overseas experienced connectivity problems resulting from the loss of fiber-optic lines that ran through Manhattan and the temporary disruption of access to Manhattan-based services. (The experience of these networks and providers offers insights into how to plan for future incidents.)

- *Surges in demand for some Internet services.* As word of the attacks began to spread, Internet users turned to a variety of news sites for more information. The greatly increased load on these sites made it difficult for all requests to be met.

COLLAPSE OF NORTH AND SOUTH TOWERS

Internet facilities were destroyed when the World Trade Center's Twin Towers collapsed. Several ISPs, including AT&T Local Systems, Genuity, Verizon, and WorldCom, had points of presence (POPs)—facilities at which customers are connected to an ISP's network—located in the Trade Center complex. Also, a number of fiber-optic cables ran through the complex in conduits, and circuits of one major telecommunications carrier ran through the Port Authority Trans-Hudson (PATH) sub-site rail tubes that link Manhattan and New Jersey. MFN alone reported the loss of more than 1,300 optical fibers as a result of the towers' collapse.

Building 7 Collapse and Damage to Verizon Central Office

At approximately 3:45 P.M., ISPs received reports of a fire in or near the Verizon central office at 140 West Street. From a local perspective, the biggest effects probably came from the collapse of Building 7 of the Trade

Center complex at about 5:20 P.M.; this collapse caused extensive damage in Verizon's central office, across the street at 140 West Street, crushing the walls and cable vaults and causing the office to begin to flood. The result was disrupted service over the course of the evening. Some 14,000 business and 20,000 residential customers lost telephone service (approximately 300,000 voice circuits). Data communications, with a total capacity equivalent to 3.6 million 56 kilobit-per-second (kbps) circuits (or 90 OC 48 SONET links), were also disrupted. Ultimately, all customers directly connected to equipment located at West Street lost Internet service. Several competitive local exchange carriers (CLECs) and ISPs also had equipment in the West Street building, and service in their networks was affected as well.

Damage to 140 West Street also caused further damage to fiber links already compromised by the collapse of the Twin Towers. In some cases the fiber-optic infrastructure had self-healed by routing around the damage done by the Towers' collapse; the SONET fiber-optic rings commonly used for metropolitan-area networks can be configured to automatically recover in the event of a single cut in the ring. But the infrastructure was not designed to heal from a second break in the fiber.

As a result of these events, Internet connectivity to several universities, medical colleges, and hospitals, and to the city government's official Web site, was interrupted. ISPs took a number of steps to restore connectivity, as described below.

Electrical Power at Co-location Sites in Lower Manhattan

In addition to the direct effects from the collapse of the Twin Towers and Building 7, there were indirect effects of the attacks, especially regarding electrical power. These disruptions had consequences for other critical telecommunications facilities, even those located outside the area of the attacks' direct physical impacts.

To be sure, telecommunications facilities operators make provisions for power failures. ISP co-location facilities and telephone central offices contain backup batteries and generators. The exact battery time and fuel capacity of individual offices is not public information, but they generally are provisioned for between 8 and 72 hours of backup in case of commercial electric-utility failure.

Most facilities routinely test their backup systems to ensure that they work. However, it is still not uncommon for a backup system to fail to start up correctly when regular power fails.[2] Still, by 4:35 P.M., several

---

[2]Participants at the committee's meeting in Washington, D.C., estimated that backup systems fail to start correctly in about 1 out of 10 tests.

Internet co-location facilities near the World Trade Center complex were operating on backup generators because commercial utility power had failed or been turned off (by Consolidated Edison, the local electric utility).

Luckily enough, the backup power systems at all the co-location and phone facilities in Lower Manhattan apparently turned on properly when Consolidated Edison was forced to turn off power just before 10:00 P.M. on September 11. However, as the power outage extended over multiple days (past the planned life of the backup power systems), maintaining power became a serious issue as batteries expired and backup generators ran out of fuel.

Following the loss of the grid electricity supply, some fiber-optic links, which depend on electrically powered termination devices at each end for sending and receiving pulses of light over the fiber, failed. It is standard practice to attach these devices to batteries, which provide several hours of backup power. However, several providers apparently failed to antici-pate significantly longer power outages, such as providing additional backup using electrical generators. Consequently, in the early morning of September 12, some minor perturbations in Internet connectivity occurred in the New York City area when the backup batteries supplying optical devices ran out of power themselves.

Although power problems did not persist beyond the month of Sep-tember 2001, some longer-term effects may still remain. In particular, some networking equipment in the area around the World Trade Center site may have sustained damage from overheating, caused by the loss of power to cooling systems and excessive dust in the air conditioning. One concern from such incidents is that the affected equipment, though still operating, could be less reliable in the future.

INTERNET-WIDE (GLOBAL) PHENOMENA

Routing and Reachability

Changes in routing information exchanged using the Border Gate-way Protocol (BGP) indicate changes to the Internet Protocol (IP) routing topology (see Chapter 5 for more details). Route withdrawals (indicating that a path to a group of Internet addresses is no longer available) and advertisements (indicating how to reach a group of Internet addresses) are routine events. They occur, for example, as circuits go up and down and when network operators make changes in their networks to adjust traffic flows across different routes.

The collapse of the South Tower was the first event to cause visible effects on global routing. Figure 2.1 (prepared by Renesys Corporation, using data collected by the RIPE [Réseaux IP Européens] Network Coor-

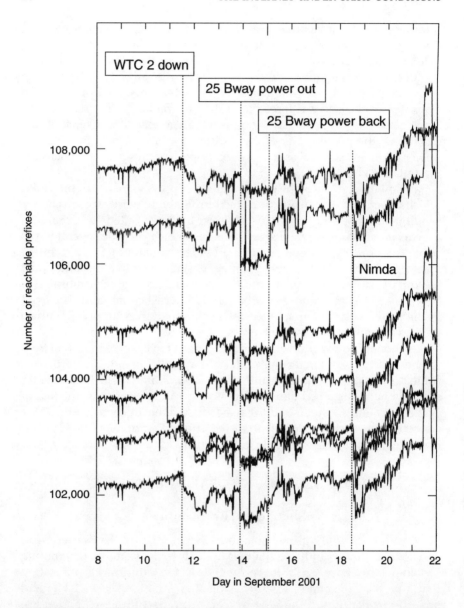

FIGURE 2.1 Number of reachable network prefixes as reported by several BGP core routers from the United States, Europe, and Japan from September 8 to September 22, 2001. (All times GMT.) Major events are marked on the plot. SOURCE: Renesys Corporation analysis of RIPE RIS archives.

dination Center from several sources) shows changes to the BGP routing table. Events are reflected in reachability measures as well: Matrix NetSystems recorded a brief 8 percent decrease in the ability to reach (ping) a select number of sites on the Internet in the minutes following the collapse of the first tower (see Figure 2.2).[3] A loss of this magnitude for an extended period of time would generally be considered a serious problem, but its occurrence for a brief period of minutes is less so—and certainly not unprecedented. Data from a full month show other dips in reachability, but of a smaller magnitude (see Figure 2.3).

Internet routing and reachability measurements returned nearly to normal within 15 minutes of the collapse of the South Tower. However, Matrix NetSystems and Telstra BGP data show that on September 11, about 1 to 2 percent of the approximately 105,000 routes did not return to normal for almost 24 hours. Some of these routes were for businesses located in the World Trade Center complex. Interestingly, others were associated with ISPs in other countries—Italy, Germany, Romania, and South Africa, for example. The collapse of the North Tower appears to have caused some transatlantic circuits to fail, and these ISPs obviously depended on their New York City links for more than just connectivity to the United States (see Box 2.1).

An analysis of the BGP message activity measured during and after September 11 shows that some global routing "events" (spikes in the volume of BGP messages) did take place because of outages caused by the attacks. However, the magnitude of these events was quite modest.

Overall, the rate of BGP routing advertisements and withdrawals suggests that the Internet was actually more stable than normal on September 11. One possible reason for this overall stability is that network operators understandably tend to avoid optional maintenance and hardware or software changes during emergencies. Anecdotal information from network operators also suggests that many operators were watching the news instead of making normal changes to their routers. The most significant traffic and routing events occurred several hours after the attacks; they resulted from damage to the Verizon central office at 140 West Street and power failures at the Telehouse 25 Broadway Internet co-location facility. Several of these events are visible in Figure 2.1.

---

[3]Different sets of hosts used by Matrix NetSystems display "normal" reachability levels of less than 100 percent because the list of hosts in each set is kept constant to enable comparisons over long intervals and some hosts on the list no longer exist.

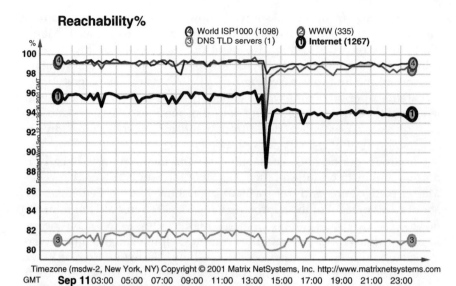

FIGURE 2.2 Reachability of four representative sets of Internet hosts on September 11, 2001. SOURCE: Matrix NetSystems, Inc.

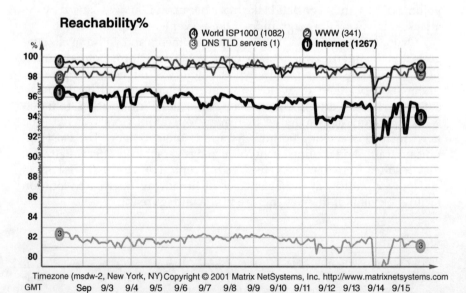

FIGURE 2.3 Reachability of four representative sets of Internet hosts during 12 days in September, 2001. SOURCE: Matrix NetSystems, Inc.

BOX 2.1
How Damaged Cables in New York City Could Affect the Internet in Other Countries

It may seem surprising that events in New York City could have disrupted Internet connectivity far from U.S. shores, but one explanation is the structure of the international telecommunications market. The pricing and availability of international phone circuits are complex and do not necessarily reflect such simple measures as distance. They do reflect such factors as treaties, other historical ties between countries, and geography. For example, it is often easier to run a cable under water than across land. Also, in many cases, it is much less expensive for an Internet service provider (ISP) in country A to connect with an ISP in neighboring country B by leasing a line to the United States (or, in some cases, to the United Kingdom) than simply by leasing a line that runs directly from A to B. As a result, many regions choose to interconnect their various ISPs in the United States. New York City (and London) are key interconnection points for Africa and parts of Europe. Miami, Florida, is a major interconnection point for Central and South America. It is this counterintuitive interconnection pattern that explains why the collapse of the World Trade Center affected networks in Italy, Germany, Romania, and South Africa.

Traffic Load Across the Internet

Active ping-style probes are used by a number of entities to monitor the Internet. Data from these sources showed only a small loss in overall connectivity during September 11 and a corresponding slight increase in packet delay times and loss. One example, collected by the Cooperative Association for Internet Data Analysis (CAIDA), is shown in Figure 2.4. Measurements such as these reflect a sort of global average, highlighting the fact that from a global traffic perspective, the events of September 11 were actually quite localized in scope.

These observations are supported by passive measurements of packet traffic. Reports of several ISPs that participated in the committee's workshop indicated that the total level of Internet traffic in fact dropped slightly on September 11 compared with that on the previous Tuesday. The normal Internet pattern, by contrast, is for traffic volume to increase slightly each week.

One ISP provided workshop participants with detailed information about traffic on its backbone that confirmed the general reports received from other ISPs. The ISP providing the detailed information did not experience any unusual peak traffic loads, delay, or loss within its backbone. Nor did it report any unusual routing instability there. Impacts were confined to the edges of its network, such as customer-access lines. This view is supported by data from Yahoo, which averaged roughly 1

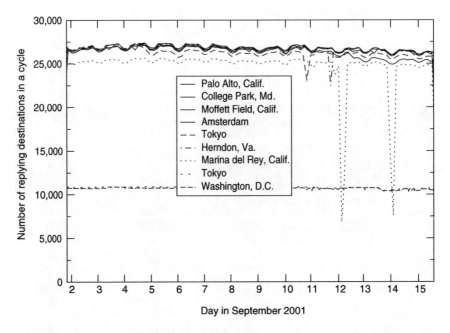

FIGURE 2.4 Reachability seen by various CAIDA monitors in September 2001.
SOURCE: CAIDA.

billion page views per day at that time. Traffic to news sites jumped
threefold on September 11, and queries related to a search for news
jumped 50-fold; yet the overall traffic was just slightly lower than normal.

Not all ISPs reported lower traffic levels, however. Some that special-
ize in content delivery (i.e., ISPs that combine regional or national networks and high-performance Web servers to provide high-performance
Web hosting) saw a large increase in traffic. One nationwide content-
distribution network (Akamai) saw traffic jump 350 percent above normal, likely reflecting increased interest on September 11 in particular content, such as news images, and additional use of its service by some major
content providers.

Another measure of Internet use is the rate at which dial-up users log
in to their ISPs. Consistent with reports that overall traffic declined, data
from America Online (AOL) show log-ins on September 11 falling below
the rate on September 10 during the period immediately following the
plane crashes and during the evening hours (see Figure 2.5). Two plausible explanations are that Internet news sites were experiencing high
congestion levels and that users were watching television to obtain news
and information.

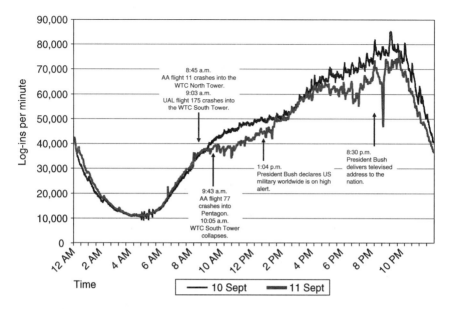

FIGURE 2.5 AOL log-ins per minute on September 10 and September 11, 2001.
SOURCE: Geraldine MacDonald, America Online.

Domain Name System

Not all Internet applications and services were affected significantly by the crisis. An example is the Domain Name System (DNS)—an important Internet service that looks up a name (e.g., <www.example.com>) in its databases and returns the Internet Protocol address (e.g., 190.0.34.72) associated with that name.[4] This process is known as name resolution. Measurements of DNS activity during September 11 show that the load on the root servers was normal to light—most likely because caching of domain names on end-hosts is typically very effective in reducing load on the system, especially when most users are accessing commonly requested sites during a crisis event. There was, however, a DNS problem in South Africa stemming from the loss of connectivity in New York, as described in the following section.

SPECIFIC NONLOCAL EFFECTS

As noted earlier, the damage around the World Trade Center complex had impacts worldwide. In addition to interruptions in local ISPs'

---

[4]W. Stevens. 1994. *TCP/IP Illustrated, Vol. 1: The Protocols*. Addison-Wesley, Boston.

connectivity to the rest of the Internet, there were more complex—and surprising—effects on the connectivity of providers, some of them located well outside New York City. These effects, resulting from subtle interdependencies between different systems and protocols, included dial-up access problems for ISPs with POPs located in New York City; loss of connectivity for networks in such disparate places as Romania and at the European Organization for Nuclear Research (CERN) in Geneva, Switzerland; and DNS problems in South Africa. Several of these problems are detailed below.

Difficulties Accessing POPs

ISPs that offer dial-up connectivity must provide several facilities, including modem banks and POPs. Customers prefer to make a local (nontoll) call to connect to their ISPs, so the providers seek to have modem banks in most local calling areas. Once connected through a modem bank, customers must authenticate themselves with the ISP before being connected to the Internet or allowed to use ISP-provided services such as e-mail or customer-created Web pages. Building a network that provides these capabilities in each local calling area is expensive and hard to maintain, so it is common practice for ISPs to simply connect a set of modem banks to a single POP (a practice known as backhauling, because the ISP "hauls the data back" to a common point). In this way, the equipment required at each modem bank is kept to a minimum. Because such POPs often cover several states or even a larger region, and because several providers' POPs for the northeastern United States happened to be located in New York City, some customers in other states found that even though they could establish a dial-up connection, they could not connect to the Internet. Their local modem banks, unbeknownst to them, were connected to a New York City POP that was out of service.

Disruption of the DNS in South Africa

Internet disruptions in New York City led to at least one protocol-related delayed reaction—disruption of DNS service—far away. Some users in South Africa reported difficulty resolving domain names ending in .za, the top-level domain for South Africa, in the days following September 11. As a result, they could not access Internet services (such as Web servers) within the country, despite the fact that there were no physical network disruptions in South Africa itself at that time.

The answer to how this happened even though networks and DNS servers in South Africa continued to operate lies in the design of the DNS. To reduce the load on name servers, the DNS supports automatic caching of frequently used names, allowing common requests to be handled with information in caches operated by a user's ISP. Only requests that are not cached are passed to higher-level servers, and if no cached information is found, ultimately the request is passed to the DNS's root servers. However, this caching does not completely isolate these users from loss of connectivity with the root servers. To ensure that updated information propagates throughout the Internet, DNS entries have an expiration date associated with them. Once an entry expires, a cache flushes the stored information and requests a fresh copy. If the root server cannot be reached, this flushed information cannot be restored.

Interdependency in Hospital Wireless Networks

Another surprising problem resulted from the loss of Internet connectivity in several hospitals. Today, many hospitals rely on handheld computers and wireless connectivity to provide doctors with bedside access to hospital databases (for receiving updated laboratory reports, for example). It turns out that by contracting with an outside carrier to provide this wireless connectivity, the hospitals introduced a dependence on Internet links. Thus if the Internet link between the hospital and the wireless carrier fails, the wireless devices will lose access even to internal databases.

Surmounting interdependencies such as these is important, because they can lead to surprising failure modes, and it is difficult—because interdependencies can arise from effects ordinarily hidden by the layered structure of the Internet architecture, or by the tendency of commercial Internet services to keep private (for competitive reasons) the specifics about their underlying interconnection structures. These interdependencies can become even more difficult to comprehend in the face of technologies that complicate the basic structure of Internet connectivity, such as virtual private networks, private address realms interconnected using network address translators, overlay networks, firewalls, or transparent proxies. In some cases, such technologies make interconnection easier by hiding internal details of the networks. At the same time, their presence can complicate interconnection by imposing additional hurdles that must be negotiated beyond the basic Internet Protocol connectivity.

RESTORATION EFFORTS

Despite the physical destruction in New York City on September 11, Internet connectivity was quickly restored for many of the affected institutions. Probably the most enduring image of data-communications restoration was the tremendous effort to put the New York Stock Exchange "back in business." But a number of other efforts to restore Internet connectivity were mounted rapidly. These activities, which involved the use of alternate paths to the Internet as well as the rapid deployment of new infrastructure, were usually less visible and more improvised, though generally effective.

ISP Cooperation

As the events of September 11 unfolded, many Internet service providers took steps to ensure that their networks would continue to run smoothly. Their actions ranged from increasing staff at network operations centers to coordinating with other ISPs to assure connectivity.

Ordinarily competitive service providers cooperated to restore connectivity lost after Verizon's 140 West Street facility was damaged. For example, NYSERNet (a nonprofit networking consortium) and Applied Theory (a for-profit spin-off of NYSERNet) reconfigured routers, shared their circuits, and made use of other circuits as far away as Buffalo, New York, to restore service to medical institutions in New York City; this roundabout approach was necessary because the two organizations' personnel could not enter the cordoned-off area south of 14th Street to access equipment.

One result was that NYC.gov, the official New York City Web site, was back in service on September 12 at 8:22 P.M. After a few days, access restrictions in Lower Manhattan were relaxed, and NYSERNet and Applied Theory staff could enter facilities in Lower Manhattan to reconfigure capacity on other SONET rings and restore service to schools, hospitals, and city governments on Long Island. Similar cooperation was reported in London and Amsterdam as ISPs made use of interconnection facilities in those cities to reconnect networks that normally would link in New York City.

ISPs encountered some glitches as they sought to communicate with each other to coordinate their activities. The ISPs typically have the phone numbers of one another's network operations centers so that their staffs can cooperate during major outages. In most cases, these are toll-free numbers. But during the middle of the day on September 11, toll-free dialing on the WorldCom telephone network was disrupted (though the toll-free service of other major providers remained operational) as a result of link failures and an increased volume of phone calls.[5] Some ISPs then

---

[5]WorldCom estimated that 187,465 toll-free queries failed during an approximately 12-hour period, starting at 9:00 A.M. on September 11. According to WorldCom's outage report to the Federal Communications Commission: "The root cause of the problem has been isolated to message congestion between the Signal Control Points (SCPs) in West Orange,

found themselves scrambling to exchange non-toll-free numbers that they normally would not have expected to need.

Some ISPs also discovered problems with their contingency plans. Not all ISPs require that their equipment automatically restart in case of a power failure; their expectation had been that in the very rare event of both primary and backup power failure, they would be able to manually restart their systems once power was restored. But the power outage at the Telehouse facility and its location in a limited-access area made those expectations untenable. The lesson is, in fact, not new. Telephone companies and some of the more savvy ISPs already knew it. Nonetheless, the incident points to the need for all telecommunications providers to consider such contingencies and to be equipped to deal with them.

Another operational challenge faced by ISPs working to restore or maintain their networks was that of basic support for personnel. Given local business closures in the wake of the attacks and the extended shifts that staff were required to work, some ISPs found it difficult to obtain food service for them.

Improvising to Restore Connectivity

In a number of cases, improvised links allowed connectivity to be restored. Some of these efforts relied on the Internet's architecture, which is compatible with almost any sort of communications link and accommodates almost any sort of service. For example:

• Wireless data links using unlicensed spectrum were used to reestablish customer connectivity from sites in Lower Manhattan to sites slightly farther north, where Internet links were undamaged.
• Time Warner Cable (TWC) deployed cable modem service to provide connectivity in state and local government offices. For example, when WNYW (Fox) and Police Plaza lost their digital subscriber line (DSL) connections, TWC replaced the Internet connectivity with Road Runner cable modem service. TWC also supplied New York City's morgue with

---

New Jersey, Dominguez Hills, California, and Irving, Texas and the switch network resulting from a mass calling event following the terrorist attacks in New York and Washington, D.C. Multiple link failures contributed to the congestion. As a result of the congestion, SCP Servers were intermittently unable to respond to queries, causing toll free service calls from the switch network to time out and fail." (WorldCom. 2001. *Final Service Disruption Report*, No. 01-149. WorldCom, Washington, D.C., October 11. Available online at <http://www.fcc.gov/Bureaus/Engineering_Technology/Filings/Network_Outage/2001/reports/01-149.pdf>.)

static IP addresses so that it could create its own networks, and cable and Road Runner service were installed at the Staten Island Red Cross. Voice-over-IP (VoIP) phones running over the cable network were used to support communications among city and state offices.[6]

• Internet phones were used in New York City as a way of circumventing problems with the local and long-distance phone networks. Organizations making these facilities available included local universities (chiefly for their students), Time Warner, and Cisco.

• In Washington, D.C., a temporary IP infrastructure was deployed at the old Naval Research Laboratory facility to provide communications services for the Department of Defense units from the Pentagon.

In addition, many users communicated using unconventional means. Institutions that had lost network connectivity were given the temporary use of other offices with Internet access through the generosity of other companies and universities.

Also, once it was discovered by the late afternoon of September 11 that making long-distance calls was often easier in New York City than placing local calls, ISPs began to advise residents having difficulty dialing into their Internet service providers to make long-distance phone calls in order to reach modems in other locations. Anecdotal accounts suggest that a large number of people did just that.

THE EXPERIENCES OF OTHER COMMUNICATIONS NETWORKS: TELEPHONE, WIRELESS VOICE AND DATA, AND BROADCASTING

The Internet was only one of several communications systems affected by the events of September 11. To place its experience in context, this section provides a brief overview of the other communications networks' efforts that day.

Telephone

As an indication of how quickly news travels (and a testament to how well the communications infrastructure was working), changes came swiftly. Apparently the first communications impact outside New York City occurred right after United Airlines Flight 175 struck the South Tower at 9:02 A.M., as the load on some telephone switches in northern New

---

[6]"World Trade Center Tragedy: Time Warner Cable of New York City & NY1 News Efforts." Time Warner Cable News Release, September 14, 2001.

Jersey impaired parts of the national toll-free calling system (discussed above, in the context of ISP coordination). Because of congestion, the Government Emergency Telecommunication System, which provides authorized users with priority access to telephone circuits, was employed by government officials. By about 9:15 A.M., the situation was quite exceptional. In New York City, call volumes were making it increasingly difficult to call into or out of the city.

Outside the city, the impact was more muted. With the exception of some difficulty with toll-free numbers, the telephone network was working well (although the load was higher than normal). The crash of American Airlines Flight 77 into the Pentagon at 9:37 A.M. did not dramatically change this picture, except to increase call volume into and out of the Washington, D.C., area, thereby adding the nation's capital to the list of difficult-to-call places. About the same time, as it was learned that the two New York planes had originated in Boston, call loads in Boston also grew.

At noon, telephone traffic remained high. Indeed, the number of telephone calls reported to have been completed by Verizon on September 11 was approximately double that of a typical day. However, it appears that difficulties in calling out of New York City may have eased by then—for example, AOL recommended that users unable to connect to its New York modem banks with a local number try calling a long-distance access number to get online; this advice apparently worked for many users.

At 5:20 P.M., World Trade Center Building 7 collapsed, severely damaging Verizon's 140 West Street central office. Although some of the equipment in the building continued to run for several more hours, local telephone connectivity through the exchange was ultimately lost. Unfortunately, the damage to the building included the disabling of some of the monitoring equipment, so it is not possible to determine exactly how telephone service degraded over the evening of September 11. Another effect of the damage to 140 West Street was to further damage fiber links already affected by the collapse of the Twin Towers, causing additional connectivity losses.

Cellular Telephones

As word of the attacks spread, the cellular telephone system in the northeastern United States began to be heavily loaded. Nationally, call volume rose 50 percent above normal. One can compare this rate with the 30 percent increase typical on Mother's Day, the canonical example of an exceptional calling day. Cellular telephone systems are usually engineered to support traffic during busy hours with only about 4 percent of calls being blocked (given a busy signal).

Regionally, the experience was even more dramatic. New York City had a 400 percent increase in call attempts during the day. At about 11:00 A.M., the volume was up 1,300 percent for at least one major carrier. Washington, D.C., had a 125 percent increase for the day. New England as a whole saw a 75 percent increase. The cellular system was not engineered for these loads, so call-blocking rates grew accordingly. In New York, 75 percent of calls were blocked (92 percent at the morning peak). In Washington, D.C., 56 percent of calls were blocked.

Wireless Internet—using such devices as Research in Motion's Blackberry—also rose on September 11. Traffic surged by 60 percent around 10:00 A.M. and stayed high through the early afternoon.[7]

Although there have been reports that a large number of cellular phone sites were disabled by the collapse of the Twin Towers, the industry maintains that only five sites were damaged in the attacks. In any case, by late afternoon on September 11, a combination of damage to telephone lines and the loss of power caused 160 cell sites in Lower Manhattan to become inoperable (slightly under 5 percent of the New York City cellular infrastructure). Over the hours and days that followed, the cellular operators adopted a variety of measures, such as the installation of temporary sites and the use of alternate radio frequencies, to restore (or in some cases, such as at the Pennsylvania crash site, to increase) capacity. In Lower Manhattan, full capacity was restored within a week.[8]

Broadcast Television and Radio

Transmission facilities of 9 of the 14 local-area television stations, along with those of 5 local radio stations, were lost when the North Tower of the World Trade Center was destroyed. Of the stations that lost their transmission facilities, only 2 were able to quickly restore service—WCBS-TV (Channel 2), which switched to a full-power backup antenna at the Empire State Building, and WXTV (Channel 41). For households that subscribed to cable, there was much less impact: most television stations deliver their feeds to cable operators directly, by way of fiber or microwave links, and the New York cable-system operators reported no service interruptions outside Lower Manhattan. (However, the impact on broad-

---

[7]From reports by carriers to the Federal Communications Commission.

[8]Data from Kathryn Condello, 2001, "Wireless Industry: Impact and Recovery Efforts Summary Report" (presentation to the Network Reliability and Interoperability Council), Cellular Telecommunications and Internet Association, Washington, D.C., October 30.

cast viewers was greater in New York City than it might have been in other metropolitan areas, as household cable penetration is only about 50 percent, significantly less than the nationwide average of 70 percent.)

To speed the restoration of broadcast service, the Federal Communications Commission gave stations temporary authority to locate replacement transmitters at any reasonable site, provided they would not cause interference with other stations' activities. Shortly after the World Trade Center buildings collapsed, a number of broadcasters set up transmitters at a tower in Alpine, New Jersey. Since then, six networks have relocated transmitters to the Empire State Building, and two have remained at the Alpine site. Broadcasters do not consider this pair of sites adequate, however, for the long term: the Empire State Building does not have enough physical or electrical capacity for all of the broadcasters, and the Alpine tower, by virtue of its relatively modest height and remote location, does not serve as sizable a market as the World Trade Center site did. Efforts are now under way to select one or more permanent transmitter sites that are more suitable.

3

The User Experience

IMPACT ON BUSINESS IN THE IMMEDIATE AREA

Wall Street-area financial institutions were of course significantly affected by the September 11 attacks, though in varying degrees. Some companies were severely hurt—Cantor Fitzgerald, for example, lost a majority of its employees and all of its facilities in the World Trade Center. Other firms suffered primarily from the loss of their physical offices. At Morgan Stanley, most employees escaped the area before the Twin Towers collapsed, but the firm's offices, along with all the information technology (IT) equipment in place there, were completely destroyed.

Other companies located near the World Trade Center, such as Merrill Lynch and Lehman Brothers Holdings, Inc., also could be categorized as "headquarters rendered unusable";[1] and a great deal of additional space in the areas abutting Ground Zero was rendered either temporarily or permanently out of commission. The New York Stock Exchange itself was shut down for almost a week, in part because many firms did not have the communications capability for completing trades and in part because the Exchange had communications and physical-damage issues of its own to contend with.

Some financial firms faced power and communications disruptions even though their office space and IT infrastructure had not been directly

---

[1]Randall Smith. 2001. "At Morgan Stanley, Readiness Saved Lives," *Wall Street Journal*, September 14, p. C1.

damaged. Most significant for companies in Lower Manhattan, the collapse of Building 7 of the World Trade Center and the consequent damage to Verizon's central office across the street disrupted voice and data lines that linked Wall Street to the world.[2] Another nearby Verizon office that served the New York Stock Exchange was also affected, with 20 percent of its high-speed data lines "out of action" and the rest "operating only sporadically."[3]

Some local firms reported not being seriously affected. For example, the director of infrastructure at Blackwood Trading LLC was quoted as saying that "if he hadn't seen the attack, he wouldn't have known it happened." Blackwood was relatively well prepared for such a disaster: while its data center is housed on Wall Street, the firm backs up all its trade data to remote centers in New Jersey, which is on a separate power grid; it was able to execute more than a "half-million trades before the NASDAQ voluntarily shut down," according to that executive.[4] Indeed, data loss was less of a problem than one might think. Most large Wall Street firms had responded to the earlier World Trade Center bombing (in 1993) by focusing their attention on crisis management,[5] which resulted in the institution of thorough data-backup or co-location procedures. Cantor Fitzgerald's eSpeed, for example, had mirrored the firm's entire operations at other sites.[6]

PEOPLE ON THE NET

Data on people's usage of the Internet following the terrorist attacks came from a variety of sources. Probably the most detailed information available to the committee was from the Pew Internet and American Life

---

[2]Shawn Tully. 2001. "Rebuilding Wall Street," *Fortune*, Vol. 144, No. 6: pp. 92-100. Available online at <http://www.fortune.com/indexw.jhtml?channel=artcol.jhtml&doc_id=204166>.

[3]Emily Thornton et al. 2001. "The View from Ground Zero," *Business Week Online*, September 13. Available online at <http://www.businessweek.com/bwdaily/dnflash/sep2001/nf20010913_005.htm>.

[4]Mark Hall and Lucas Mearian. 2001. "IT Focus Turns to Disaster Recovery," *IDG*, September 11. Available online at <http://www.cnn.com/2001/TECH/industry/09/11/disaster.recovery.idg/index.html>.

[5]Shawn Tully. 2001. "Rebuilding Wall Street," *Fortune*, Vol. 144, No. 6: pp. 92-100. Available online at <http://www.fortune.com/indexw.jhtml?channel=artcol.jhtml&doc_id=204166>.

[6]Edward Cone and Sean Gallagher. 2001. "Cantor Fitzgerald—Forty-Seven Hours," *Baseline*, October 29. Available online at <http://www.baselinemag.com/article/0,3658,apn=2&s=2101&a=17022&ap=1,00.asp>.

Project, which surveyed Internet users immediately after September 11.[7]
The project had been conducting telephone surveys of Internet users for
some time before the crisis, and it continues surveying users even now;
thus its data not only present a picture of how users behaved that day but
also allow comparison with their behavior both before and after the attack.

Other useful sources of data on user behavior included Web-usage
measurements from Webhancer, search statistics from major search sites
such as AOL and Google, and data from content providers such as
CNN.com and Akamai. Together, these data provide a very telling por-
trait of what people wanted, needed, and expected from the Internet in
those extraordinary circumstances.

The Internet as a Source of News

Many people learned of the terrorist attacks on the World Trade Center and the Pentagon while they were at work or on their way to work.[8]
And because people often do not have access to television sets at their
place of work, there is reason to believe that they then turned to Internet
news sites for information.

In what is sometimes referred to as a "flash crowd"[9] event, national
and international demand for timely information soared, and many news
Web servers—those of CNN, MSNBC, and the New York Times, for example—experienced unprecedented loads. An anecdote regarding CNN's
Web site <www.cnn.com> gives a vivid example of just how fast the
demand for Internet-accessible news grew. When the director of the facility saw on TV that the second plane had just struck, he stood up in his
cubicle and shouted to other staff members to take steps (such as bringing
extra servers online) to prepare for an increased demand for news. By the
time he sat down, that spike had already arrived. (Box 3.1 discusses the
CNN experience, including steps that the network took to keep up with
demand, in more detail.)

---

[7]Lee Raime and Bente Kalsnes. 2001. *The Commons of the Tragedy: How the Internet Was
Used by Millions After the Terror Attacks to Grieve, Console, Share News, and Debate the Country's
Response.* Pew Internet & American Life Project, Washington, D.C., October 10. Available
online at <http://www.pewinternet.org/reports/toc.asp?Report=46>.

[8]While it is difficult to get a precise estimate, data from the Census Bureau suggest that
almost half of the U.S. workforce was at work or en route when the planes hit. Information
available online at <http://www.bls.gov/news_release/flex.t07.htm>.

[9]The term "flash crowd" was coined by science fiction writer Larry Niven, who wrote a
short story by that title about masses of people teleporting to see exciting events they see
reported in the news.

During the remainder of the month after September 11, the number of Internet users who sought to get news online increased by about 25 percent, even though Internet use for some other purposes (such as shopping or sending e-mail) declined. Indeed, survey data indicate that the total number of Internet users declined by about 10 percent in the week immediately following September 11 (see Table 3.1).

Even given the surge in demand for online news, all the evidence is that Internet users, in the same proportion as the general population, preferred to get their news from television. A poll by the Pew Project showed that in the week after September 11, television was the main source of information for 79 percent of Americans and for 80 percent of the heaviest Internet users (see Table 3.2). Heavy Internet users relied on the Internet as much as on radio and newspapers, while Americans overall relied on the radio and newspapers far more than they depended on the Internet.

One possible reason for this seeming contradiction—high online demand for news *and* high reliance of Internet users on television—is that once they were home from work (where they relied largely on the Internet) on September 11, most people turned on their television sets and got the latest news without having to go online for further information. Another possible reason was frustration with the Internet: 43 percent of Internet users reported at least some trouble accessing Web sites in the first hours after the attacks, and 15 percent reported great difficulties.[10] Yet another possible reason is that news organizations generally do not provide live streaming video programming.[11] In the end, about a fifth of those who had difficulty reaching a site gave up on using the Internet for news during that period.[12]

Another important point is that many people appear to have used the Internet not as a replacement for regular news sources but as a supplement. Major search engines reported that the information sought by users changed dramatically on September 11 and in the following days. For example, on September 12, a number of talk shows mentioned Nostradamus, a Renaissance writer renowned for his prophecies. Thereafter, "Nostradamus" was at the top of the list or near the top at many popular search engines; at Yahoo, for example, it was number 1.[13] Google

---

[10]Raime and Kalsnes, 2001, *The Commons of the Tragedy*.

[11]A scalable technology known as multicast could support streaming video to large numbers of viewers, but it is not commonly employed by content providers.

[12]Raime and Kalsnes, 2001, *The Commons of the Tragedy*.

[13]Google <http://www.google.com/press/zeitgeist/9-11-search.html>; Yahoo <http://websearch.about.com/gi/dynamic/offsite.htm?site=http://buzz.yahoo.com/>; Lycos <http://websearch.about.com/gi/dynamic/offsite.htm?site=http://50.lycos.com/091101%5FSpecial.html>.

BOX 3.1
CNN.com on September 11, 2001

September 11, 2001, has certainly not been the only high-demand period experienced by Internet news sites. For example, interest in the results of the 2000 general election fueled a steep rise in demand. But September 11 set new records, and consequently the ability to reach major news Web sites that day was reduced for some people.[1]

To use this experience to better understand the demands on news servers during a crisis event and to identify measures that can help deal with that demand, a representative from CNN's Internet division was invited to participate in the workshop held by the Committee on the Internet Under Crisis Conditions. Key elements of CNN's experience follow.

On September 11, CNN's overall demand surged greatly, with the measured daily load (as expressed in page views) increasing on September 11 to 132 million—nearly 10 times the more typical load of 14 million on September 10. The measured demand of September 11 probably underestimates total user demand, however, because not all users were able to successfully load the Web page as the demand initially surged after the crash of the first airplane. The number of hits (pages or images requested) doubled every 7 minutes, resulting in an order-of-magnitude increase in less than 30 minutes. Demand for news continued to grow in the hours following the attack, with the load on September 12 reaching 304 million page views—more than twice that measured on September 11.

Keeping up with demand after the first airplane crash was very challenging for the CNN operations staff, who employed a combination of several techniques to deal with the load:

- *Reducing Web page complexity.* The CNN.com main Web page was significantly reduced in size (i.e., as measured by the number of separate elements such as

---

reported that "Nostradamus," "cnn," and "World Trade Center" were the top three terms among people whose search-engine usage increased during the week ending September 13.[14]

The Internet as a Means of Communicating Between Individuals

On September 11, many people felt the need to communicate right away with family, friends, and colleagues. The purpose of these communications ranged from emergency responses (as officials in New York

---

[14]Google. 2002. "Google Search Statistics from 9/11/01," Google, Mountain View, Calif. Available online at < http://www.google.com/press/zeitgeist/9-11-search.html>.

headline pictures and graphical menu bars for selecting additional content), consistent with CNN's in-place strategy for handling high-demand periods. In fact, the main page was stripped down to the bare bones—even further than the usual minimum—to increase its ability to serve pages. Indeed, at its minimum complexity, the page could fit into a single IP packet.

• *Adding more servers.* A number of other server systems are colocated with the servers assigned to CNN.com. These systems, which normally are used for other CNN and Turner Broadcasting content, were for the most part experiencing significantly reduced volume that day. Thus, a number of them were reconfigured and added to the CNN.com server pool. (Interestingly, CNN did retain server capacity for the Cartoon Network, which saw an increase in volume—likely reflecting parents' desire to provide children with an alternative to the disturbing news.)

• *Temporarily employing a third-party content-distribution network.* CNN arranged to significantly increase its use of the Akamai content delivery network in order to reduce the load on the CNN servers themselves. That is, the CNN Web pages temporarily pointed Web browsers to retrieve images from Akamai servers instead of from the usual CNN systems.

The net effect of all of these efforts was to enable overall capacity to increase over an order of magnitude within hours of the event, permitting CNN to cope with the greatly increased demand.

---

[1]For example, according to a report in *ComputerWorld*, the Web-measuring company Keynote observed that the availability (responsiveness to requests to download Web pages) of the Web sites of CNN, the New York Times, ABC News, MSNBC, and USA Today were all significantly reduced following 9:00 a.m. on September 11. (Todd R. Weiss. September 11, 2001. "News Sites Simplified After Performance Bogs Down." *ComputerWorld.* Available online at <www.computerworld. com/managementtopics/ebusiness/story/0,10801,63729,00.html>.)

City and Washington, D.C., sought to deal with the crisis) to trying simply to make sense of what was happening.

Although the Internet was one medium by which people chose to communicate, it is important to emphasize that the preferred mode of personal communications was the telephone. Indeed, even heavy Internet users reported using the telephone more than the Internet (and at a higher rate than the national average). While 63 percent of Americans phoned a family member about the attacks on September 11 or in the following days, 75 percent of heavy Internet users called a family member during that period.[15]

---

[15]Raime and Kalsnes, 2001, *The Commons of the Tragedy.*

TABLE 3.1 Internet Use by Activity, August Through September 2001

Activity	Aug. 13–Sept. 10[a] (percentage)	Sept. 12–19[b] (percentage)	Sept. 20–Oct. 1[c] (percentage)
Going online for any purpose	56	51	57
Sending or reading e-mail	51	42	49
Getting news online	22	27	26
Seeking hobby information	20	10	22
Browsing for fun	20	13	20
Doing work-related research	17	13	15
Seeking medical or health information	5	3	5
Buying products	4	2	2

[a]N = 1,351; margin of error is ±3 percent.
[b]N = 1,138; margin of error is ±3 percent.
[c]N = 525; margin of error is ±6 percent.
SOURCE: Lee Raime and Bente Kalsnes. 2001. *The Commons of the Tragedy: How the Internet Was Used by Millions After the Terror Attacks to Grieve, Console, Share News, and Debate the Country's Response.* Pew Internet & American Life Project, Washington, D.C., October 10, p. 7. Available online at <http://www.pewinternet.org/reports/toc.asp?Report=46>.

TABLE 3.2 Main Source of Information Following September 11, 2001

Main Source of Information	All Americans[a] (percentage)	Heaviest Internet Users[b] (percentage)
Television	79	80
Radio	7	6
Newspaper	7	7
Internet	2	6
Talking with others	2	1

[a]N = 1,029; margin of error is ±3 percent.
[b]N = 260; margin of error is ±7 percent. The Pew study defines the heaviest Internet users as those who have more than 3 years' experience online and who log on from home every day. This group constitutes about 20 percent of all Internet users and about 11 percent of the U.S. adult population
SOURCE: Lee Raime and Bente Kalsnes. 2001. *The Commons of the Tragedy: How the Internet Was Used by Millions After the Terror Attacks to Grieve, Console, Share News, and Debate the Country's Response.* Pew Internet & American Life Project, Washington, D.C., October 10, p. 10. Available online at <http://www.pewinternet.org/reports/toc.asp?Report=46>.

At the same time, about one-third of Americans had difficulty placing a phone call on September 11 (see "The Experiences of Other Communications Networks" in Chapter 2 for more detail on the telephone system and its performance), and about one in eight turned to the Internet to communicate with friends and loved ones. Much of the communication was through e-mail, which was used almost as soon as the attacks began, though a modest fraction of Internet users (13 percent) reported using instant messages.[16] Anecdotal reports both from Washington, D.C., and New York City suggest that instant messaging proved a viable alternative for office workers who were unable to use their phones but still had Internet access.

Those directly affected by the attacks also made use of Internet communications. Some people trapped at the top of the Twin Towers were able to e-mail colleagues and family.[17] Some communications from the Twin Towers were from people who used wireless PDAs, such as those from Research in Motion (Blackberry), to send messages even after in-building infrastructure had been knocked out.

Finally, Internet telephony provided a useful alternative communications channel for some people who had lost telephone service, though apparently the total number of such calls was small compared to those placed through the conventional telephone network.

The Internet and Community

In the hours and days following the attacks, a number of Web sites were created (or adapted from existing sites) to help fill various disaster-related needs. They included the following:

• *Missing person and "I'm alive" lists.* For example, Prodigy Communications created an "I'm ok" online message center to help people find information about loved ones.
• *Relief supply requests.*
• *Solicitations for relief contributions.* Companies such as Amazon.com and Yahoo used their Internet billing systems to facilitate people's donations to the American Red Cross.

---

[16]Raime and Kalsnes, 2001, *The Commons of the Tragedy.*
[17]*New York Times.* 2002. "Fighting to Live as the Towers Died." May 26, p. 1, col. 1.

Overall Use of the Internet

Total use of the Internet declined, as discussed above. (Instances in which particular ISPs instead saw a rise in traffic levels appear to be attributable to their serving news and other content that were in higher demand on September 11.) The decrease in overall demand is apparent in both the Pew Internet users survey data and in reports of ISPs, including presenters at the workshop.

4

Perspectives on the Internet Experience of September 11

The overall events of September 11 were so extraordinary and shocking that it is sometimes difficult to put them in perspective. There is a tendency to look for echoes of the Twin Towers' fall in everything one sees. This chapter seeks to provide some of that perspective by examining other major communications events occurring on the Internet and seeing how they compared. Then it considers what could happen to the Internet if attacked directly (rather than suffering collateral damage) or if it were used as an integral part of the attack itself.

OTHER OUTAGES:
OPERATOR ERRORS AND INFRASTRUCTURE FAULTS

The committee's conclusion is that September 11, with respect to its impact on the Internet, was a relatively minor incident. Yet quantifying that observation has proved difficult. There are neither general norms of Internet performance nor infrastructure to monitor the network comprehensively. Rather, individuals and organizations rate the Internet's performance differently, according to their own priorities.

Still, there are several basic measures that interested parties generally use to assess the Internet's performance:

- *Traffic levels.* How much does traffic vary from that of a typical day?
- *Border Gateway Protocol (BGP) reachability and update rates.* How

many regions of the network are being advertised by BGP, and how often is the information about various parts of the network changing?

• *Measured reachability.* Rather than relying on BGP, one can measure Internet connectivity directly by attempting to communicate with a number of systems scattered throughout the network and reporting on one's actual ability to exchange data.

In the following paragraphs, these metrics are used to examine some recent Internet events that most people consider exceptional and to compare them with those of September 11.

Operator Error

Network operators often joke that a single misplaced comma in an appropriate configuration file could take down the Internet. While that was certainly true in the late 1980s,[1] operators today have well-defined procedures and methods for checking configurations before putting them into their networks. Furthermore, most operators employ systems to protect their network from configuration errors in other networks. However, operational errors do still occur from time to time, and some of these have major effects.

To illustrate how local errors can have global impact, let us consider an example from the Domain Name System (DNS)—a distributed database that keeps the name-to-address mappings for the Internet. If a Web browser needs to find the Internet address of the name <www. nationalacademies.org>, for example, the browser queries the DNS.

The DNS is a hierarchical database that makes heavy use of caching. To explain the process by simplifying somewhat, the way that a name such as <www. nationalacademies.org> is looked up in the DNS is as follows: the browser asks a local DNS server if it knows the name <www. nationalacademies.org>. If the local server knows the name, it returns the IP address for <www.nationalacademies.org>; if not, the server consults 1 of 13 root servers. The root servers act as query managers; though they rarely answer a query themselves, they tell the local server what DNS server it should consult to get the definitive answer about <www. nationalacademies.org>.

What makes the DNS work and keeps the root servers from being overwhelmed with queries is the system's use of caching. Once a local

---

[1]In the late 1980s, the Internet often suffered from so-called black-hole problems—routers misconfigured to erroneously report to other routers that they have the best possible route to every point on the Internet. A black hole effectively encourages all nearby routers to send all traffic to it and then discards all the incoming traffic as undeliverable.

server is told the address of <www.nationalacademies.org>, it is expected to cache that address for some period of time (a few hours or days), so that the next time the server is asked about <www.nationalacademies. org> it will not have to query the root servers again. The exact time that a name is cached is controlled by the owner of the name. For example, the National Academies determine how long the name <www.national academies.org> can be cached at a server.

In February 2001, a router that connected the DNS servers for names ending in microsoft.com to the rest of the Internet was misconfigured, and the router stopped forwarding traffic. It turned out that, contrary to recommended practice, Microsoft had placed all the microsoft.com servers on the same local network; thus, when the router stopped working, no one could query about names ending in microsoft.com. Furthermore, Microsoft had decided to keep the cache times on its names very short— about 2 hours. As a result, within that time every name ending in microsoft.com effectively became unknown on the Internet.

Unfortunately, in terms of impact on the network, Microsoft names are very popular. As the DNS dropped Microsoft names from caches, any query about a Microsoft site had to be sent to the root servers, which would then point the queries at the microsoft.com servers. Because the servers were unreachable, the query would fail, no names would be cached, and the next query for a Microsoft site would again result in a query of the root servers. Loads jumped by 25 percent at some root servers until the misconfigured router was repaired.[2] In contrast, the events of September 11 had no discernible effect on the number of queries to the root servers.

Infrastructure Faults

In many ways, the effects on the Internet from the September 11 attacks were similar to other, albeit accidental, "infrastructure faults" that the Internet has incurred. Figure 4.1 illustrates the effects on the global Internet of one such type of fault, a "fiber cut," on November 23, 1999, when a major Internet link was severed. The figure plots Internet reachability using the same methodology as was used in Figure 2.2 in Chapter 2. The effects of the fiber cut are comparable to those of the September 11 damage—all in all, about a 6 to 7 percent loss in overall Internet connectivity, but short-lived. Figure 4.2 shows another outage

---

[2]Nevil Brownlee, K.C. Claffy, and Evi Nemeth. 2001. *DNS Measurements at a Root Server.* Cooperative Association for Internet Data Analysis, San Diego. Available online at <http:// www.caida.org/outreach/papers/2001/DNSMeasRoot/>.

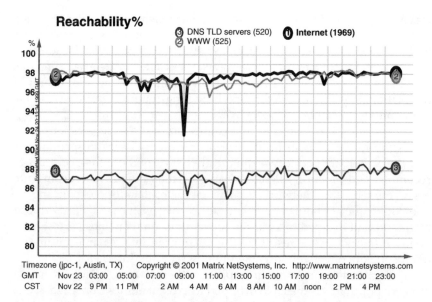

FIGURE 4.1 Impact of a 1999 fiber cut on the reachability of two representative sets of Internet hosts (1, 2) and the Domain Name System root servers (3). SOURCE: Matrix NetSystems, Inc.

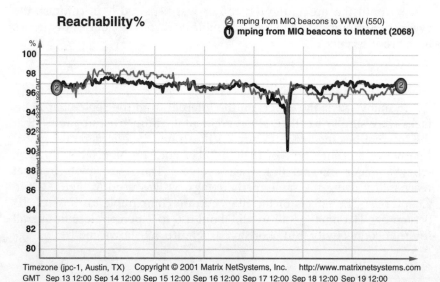

FIGURE 4.2 Impact of damage from Hurricane Floyd on the reachability of two representative sets of Internet hosts. SOURCE: Matrix NetSystems, Inc.

with similar effects but a different cause; here, the downward spikes on September 17, 1999, coincide near the peak of the physical damage inflicted by Hurricane Floyd. Again, the magnitude of the spikes are comparable with that of September 11, 2001.

ATTACKS ON, OR WITH, THE INTERNET

Baseline: Effects of Damage on September 11

On September 11, an important interconnection point (at 140 West Street in New York City) was severely damaged, some long-distance communications links (especially those under the World Trade Center complex) were severed, and there was a localized electrical power outage. Those experiences, together with discussions about them with several Internet service providers, give some indication of the Internet's vulnerability to a direct and deliberate physical attack. As detailed in Chapter 2, the effects of the terrorist attacks were complex, but by simplifying somewhat, some broad patterns emerge:

- *Most of the attacks' effects were local.* The majority of the serious communications disruptions were suffered by networks and customers—such as the stock exchanges, Covad DSL customers, and the parts of NYSERNet in Lower Manhattan—physically close to 140 West Street. Effects of the attacks were substantially less notable in Upper Manhattan, and nationally they were hard to discern at all.
- *Nonlocal effects occurred in surprising places.* Some Internet customers in western New England found that connectivity problems in New York affected their ability to dial in to their ISP. And one of the most seriously affected parts of the Internet turned out to be an ocean away—in South Africa.
- *Rich communications infrastructure and the flexibility of the Internet technology eased recovery.* While a number of address ranges were briefly removed from the Internet by the attacks, most of them were back on the network in less than a day. The rich communications infrastructure of the United States made it feasible for most ISPs to reroute around the damage. In cases where rerouting was not an option (as at locations in Lower Manhattan), it was often possible to improvise new connectivity (e.g., a IEEE 802.11b wireless link extending out a window in New York City). Oversimplifying a little, it was only sites within a few blocks of the World Trade Center or sites with limited communications infrastructure (e.g., some of the non-U.S. areas affected by the collapse) that had difficulty recovering. And even in many of the difficult cases, recovery time was still measured in days (not weeks or months).

• *Long power outages caused serious harm to communications.* One can argue that, from the perspective of the Internet, the most serious effect of the attacks on the World Trade Center was that power had to be shut off to Lower Manhattan. The power outage at Telehouse had an effect on Internet connectivity that was comparable to that of the Towers' collapses earlier. Extended power outages tend to be a feature of physical disasters (whether they have human or natural causes), and they have great impact: the nation's communications infrastructure ultimately relies on powered equipment to carry data.

If the Internet Were the Target, Would There Be Greater Impact?

If attackers were out to physically damage the Internet infrastructure directly, it is unlikely that 140 West Street would be near the top of their list. Even within Manhattan, several facilities contain substantially more Internet equipment and are more important to the Internet's operation.

Many have speculated that a physical attack on one of the major Internet exchange locations, such as MAE-East (near Washington, D.C.) or the PAIX facility (near San Francisco), would cause serious disruptions. Internet exchange locations are facilities at which a number of ISPs install routers on a common network. This mode of interconnection is often more cost-effective than is arranging a separate physical connection to each network at which an ISP wishes to peer. Concern is simultaneously heightened as well: an attack on an exchange location would break multiple connections between ISPs.

But as best as the committee can determine, such an attack would not pose a serious risk to the Internet as a whole. Most ISPs are connected to it at more than one point, both to increase their redundancy in the face of unintended events—such as fiber cuts and power failures—and because they generally seek to exchange traffic with other ISPs as close as possible to the traffic's origin, thereby avoiding additions to the load on their own networks. Indeed, the largest ISPs are connected to one another at dozens of points throughout the United States. The committee finds no reason to believe that there is a point (or even a small number of points) in the Internet that, if removed, would partition the country's system into a disconnected group of networks.

Another concern is that an attacker could sever a critical fiber-optic link. However, as a matter of practice, large ISPs maintain networks with redundant paths to ensure connectivity in such circumstances. To be sure, the level of redundancy can turn out to be lower than the literal counting of links would suggest. In a number of places, fiber runs are concentrated in particular rights-of-way, as was illustrated by a 2001 incident in which a fire in a Baltimore, Maryland, train tunnel destroyed a number of links. But carriers work hard to discover such vulnerabilities, and large networks deploy geographically distinct links that allow a damaged link to be bypassed (though performance in terms of capacity or delay may suffer until that link is restored). The September 11 experience demonstrated such redundancy in major Internet links.

Indeed, it turns out that failures of one or more Internet components are not infrequent events. Fiber cuts occur often, and most major Internet exchange points have failed at one time or another. In the past, there have even been simultaneous failures of exchange points in at least three different locations. Some of these events have had noticeable effects on one or more ISPs, but the impact is not felt across the Internet. As is described in Box 4.1, the Internet's basic design makes it resilient in the face of failures—incidents do not tend to ripple across the whole network.

There is, however, some reason to believe that it might be possible for a motivated attacker to cut the Internet links between the United States and other countries; these links appear to have less redundancy than is present within the backbones of major U.S. ISPs. It is highly likely that such an attack would also separate a number of countries outside the United States from each other. Moreover, such incidents could lead to indirect effects along the lines of the degradation of South Africa's DNS capability following the World Trade Center attacks.

The principal issue with international connectivity is that most of the transoceanic fiber-optic communications cables land in North America at a few sites. As noted in Chapter 2, one reason why New York City is a superhub for the Internet is that a large number of the transatlantic cables make landfall close to the city. Similarly, Miami, Florida, is a hub for connectivity with Latin America. The vulnerability is further increased because, for economic reasons, most connections to these transoceanic cables are made at carrier hotels in New York City rather than at the landing points themselves; it is much cheaper to run one fiber-optic cable from the landing to an interconnection point than it is for each carrier wishing to connect to the fiber to run separate lines. Many of the individual landing points are themselves also vulnerable to attack.

It should also be noted that although it is difficult for a physical attack to damage the Internet as a whole, there are a number of ways to attack an individual ISP, many of which would cause problems for several hours or days. Economies of scale can be achieved by concentrating equipment in a small number of locations, and some ISPs, as well as content ISPs (which run large Web farms), seem particularly prone to doing so, even going so far as putting all their "eggs" (servers) in one "basket" (location), which obviously makes the ISP more vulnerable to physical attack. (Some ISPs

---

BOX 4.1
How the Internet's Design Makes It Resilient

The Internet differs fundamentally from most of the other communications networks in how it adapts to equipment failures and increases in traffic load, a legacy of the design goals of the early days of the ARPANET.[1] Whereas the telephone network has very complicated switches but simple "edge devices" (i.e., telephones), the Internet places much of its intelligence in the end-hosts. The network provides a relatively simple service of best-effort packet delivery. Packets flow through the network independently and may be lost, corrupted, or delivered out of order. The fact that the Internet Protocol (IP) offers such a simple packet-delivery service makes it easier to continue providing the service during transient network failures. After a failure, the network routers communicate among themselves to compute a new path, if possible, to the packet's destination. Some packets may be lost during this transition period, but the communication continues after the routers start using the new path.

Building on top of the IP, the end-hosts implement transport-layer protocols that coordinate the end-to-end delivery of data between applications. The Transmission Control Protocol (TCP) underlies most communication on the Internet, such as the downloading of Web pages. TCP provides the main mechanism needed by most Internet applications—a logical connection that delivers a sequence of bytes from the sender to the receiver in an ordered, reliable fashion—and it is used for much of the traffic over the Internet. Hosts running TCP adapt their behavior to network congestion.[2] In response to loss or delay, the TCP sender reduces the transmission rate to avoid overloading the network. During periods of heavy load, TCP senders traversing the same bottlenecked link transmit at a lower rate to share the limited resources.

This adaptability has the advantage that application performance tends to "degrade gracefully" under heavy load, though such a degradation in performance may drop to a level that is unacceptable for some users. It may be acceptable for applications such as e-mail (which can be queued and delivered as bandwidth becomes available) and instant messaging (which requires little bandwidth), but it can be disruptive for Web downloads and can unacceptably degrade multimedia streaming.

---

do operate multiple facilities, but even then, they tend to locate them within the same cluster of buildings. This strategy is not sufficiently robust, as power failures would likely cause problems across the entire complex.)

Finally, the committee learned during its workshop that a carefully designed distributed attack against a number of physical locations, especially if done in a repeating pattern, could be highly disruptive. An attack at a single point, however, is survivable.

The adaptation of the TCP to network congestion is in sharp contrast to the control mechanisms in the traditional telephone network, which determine the path for the call and allocate the necessary bandwidth before transmitting any data. For example, the telephone network dedicates 64 kilobits per second for each telephone call on each link in its route. The connection is not established unless sufficient resources are available, ensuring that existing telephone calls are not affected by the decision to accept a new connection. A disadvantage of this approach is that users may experience blocked calls (i.e., busy signals) after network failures and during periods of heavy call volume, but it has the advantage that the heavy load does not degrade the quality of ongoing phone conversations. In addition, the telephone network has mechanisms for imposing priority on which calls are accepted. For example, the network can be configured to favor outgoing calls in disaster areas to enable victims to reach the outside world.

The Internet, meanwhile, was designed for robustness and adaptivity to serve all users. Though the hardware and software components in early IP networks were not very reliable, especially in comparison with the mature technology in the telephone network, the designers of the ARPANET wanted the network to continue to function even if a natural disaster or malicious attack caused individual components to fail. These design principles enabled the Internet to withstand the localized physical attacks it endured on September 11. The attacks separated a small number of networks from the rest of the Internet, but by and large the infrastructure was able to adapt by exploiting alternate routes around the failed equipment and by having end-hosts adjust their sending rates to the available bandwidth.

---

[1]David D. Clark. 1988. "The Design Philosophy of the DARPA Internet Protocols," pp. 106-114 in *SIGCOMM '88, Proceedings of the ACM Symposium on Communications Architectures and Protocols*, August 16-18, 1988, Stanford, Calif. Association for Computing Machinery, New York, N.Y.

[2]Van Jacobson. 1988. "Congestion Avoidance and Control," *SIGCOMM '88, Proceedings of the ACM Symposium on Communications Architectures and Protocols*, August 16-18, 1988, Stanford, Calif. Association for Computing Machinery, New York, N.Y.

POSSIBLE EFFECTS OF A DELIBERATE ELECTRONIC ATTACK WITH THE AID OF, OR AGAINST, THE INTERNET

As previously noted, the Internet itself was not a target on September 11, 2001, nor, apparently, was it used by terrorists for anything more than their own information-acquisition or communication needs. However, the Internet could plausibly play a more central role in future terrorist attacks. Acquiring the expertise necessary to use it in that way would be analogous to the efforts of the September 11 attackers in learning how to pilot jet aircraft. Once the expertise was acquired, the Internet could be utilized by terrorists in a number of ways and in the pursuit of diverse goals.

The potential, range, and plausibility of terrorist attacks on or with the Internet are thoroughly explored in *Making the Nation Safer: The Role of Science and Technology in Countering Terrorism*, a recent National Research Council publication[3] to which the committee defers for a complete discussion. This section only sketches some of the possibilities for terrorist use of the Internet, primarily to develop a contrast with the actual impact *on* the Internet from September 11.

If the aim is terror, then widespread Internet failures could cause confusion and possibly instill panic, particularly if such failures occurred in conjunction with separate physical attacks. Broader attacks of *any* form could have this effect, but the Internet would prove a particularly valuable element because of its use by some as a news channel and especially because its functioning and vulnerabilities remain a mystery to much of the populace—people might fear the worst if a significant disruption to the Internet were to occur.

A different Internet-related means for instilling panic would be to create misinformation. This could be done directly, by altering the contents of Internet news sites. Alternatively, information in the Domain Name System database could be changed to redirect names to incorrect addresses, or the routing system could be tampered with so that users would be connected to substitute servers.[4] Each technique could expose users to Web pages, seemingly authentic, that contained either subtly or grossly incorrect information crafted by the attackers.

Attackers could also attempt to use the Internet either to directly inflict damage or to augment damage inflicted by other means. For example, they could undermine systems whose operations rely on using the Internet or are susceptible to manipulation through the Internet (see *Making the Nation Safer* for further discussion).

Another form of terrorist attack could involve the direct infliction of damage, by nonphysical means, on the Internet's own systems. This might be done in several ways:

---

[3]National Research Council. 2002. *Making the Nation Safer: The Role of Science and Technology in Countering Terrorism*. National Academies Press, Washington, D.C. Available online at <http://books.nap.edu/html/stct/index.html>. For an extended discussion, see the forthcoming Computer Science and Telecommunications Board report on information technology for countering terrorism.

[4]Some of the risks of DNS and routing attacks are described in Computer Science and Telecommunications Board, National Research Council. 1999. *Trust in Cyberspace*. National Academy Press, Washington, D.C.

- By the deletion of information (such an attempt might not be highly effective, however, as mechanisms exist to deal with the routine occurrence of corrupted information);
- By disabling hardware (for some machines, it is possible to use software to render the hardware inoperable); or
- By rendering services inaccessible (for example, if computers under attackers' control continually flood a service with bogus traffic).

These threats might seem minor compared to physical damage that attackers could inflict, except that the scale of such software-based attacks is potentially immense. And it is well established that attackers can acquire access to hundreds or thousands of machines to be used as launching points for coordinated follow-on attacks.

Toolkits that exist for automatically scanning and exploiting a wide variety of security flaws in Internet servers could also be used as weapons. When coupled with software that then repeats the scanning and exploiting (using each newly compromised machine as an additional platform), they become a "worm" or a virus (the distinction being that viruses require some user action to activate them, while worms do not). Though not a new concept, worms recently gained notoriety with the advent, in the summer of 2001, of Code Red and Nimda—worms that infected several hundred thousand Internet hosts in a matter of hours.

Furthermore, recent theoretical work has pointed to more efficient spreading strategies that appear to enable a worm to compromise a vulnerable population of a million servers in a matter of minutes, perhaps even in tens of seconds.[5] And a plausible potential exists for compromising perhaps 10 million Internet hosts in a surreptitious "contagion" fashion that, while taking longer than the quick propagation of worms such as Code Red, would make the worm much harder to detect; it would not exhibit the telltale scanning used by rapidly propagating worms.

The ability to acquire hundreds of thousands or even millions of hosts would enable terrorists to launch truly Internet-wide attacks. One form of attack would be distributed denial-of-service (DDOS) floods, in which an immense stream of traffic is sent to a particular Internet service or resource (such as a particular router or access link). Such attacks gained notoriety in February 2000 with a series of floods that targeted popular Internet sites such as Yahoo.

Given the state of the art in defending against such attacks, it would

---

[5]S. Staniford, V. Paxson, and N. Weaver. August 2002. "How to Own the Internet in Your Spare Time," in *Proceedings of the USENIX Security Symposium, August 5-9, 2002, San Francisco, California, USA*. USENIX Association, Berkeley, Calif.

be very difficult to deal with attacks from even a few thousand coordinated hosts. Thus a hundred or a thousand times as many hosts would utterly overwhelm any known defensive measures—with the result that attackers could launch *many* DDOS attacks simultaneously against a wide range of services. For example, they could plausibly target *all* of the root name servers (of which 13 are currently deployed and operated by various organizations) *and* all of the major Internet news outlets *and* the cybersecurity analysis and response sites. Or, they could use the machines to overwhelm the components of the public telephone network. Or they could pursue both strategies at the same time.

The skills required to launch worm-based attacks are not extremely difficult to acquire, and the damage and confusion that they would cause could be quite significant. Thus, they appear to constitute a major form of Internet threat—one for which, at present, there is little in the way of defense. However, *Making the Nation Safer* does provide recommendations on some possible countermeasures for such cyberterrorism.

5

Measuring the Internet

The information collected by the committee provided a rough picture of what occurred on and after September 11 with respect to Internet performance. The two key sources were reports from people and direct measurements of Internet systems (such as links, routers, and hosts).

The information that was available indicated some interesting contrasts between September 11 and a "typical" day. Network traffic loads measured in several ISP networks the day of the attacks were generally lighter than normal. However, demand on servers at the major news Web sites was unprecedented—to such an extent that several of these systems were rendered inoperative for a period of hours. At the same time, several measurements suggested that the impact of the events of September 11 on the Internet was modest. The effects on the network infrastructure caused by physical damage in Lower Manhattan and at the Pentagon were quite limited, and they appeared smaller, or no worse, than what would result from other incidents. For example, with respect to data on the reachability of a particular set of Internet addresses, September 11 was more or less equivalent to a fiber cut—a nontrivial but relatively routine event. These data were supplemented by other information—polls of Internet users, for example.

Measurements of Internet systems from the September 11 crisis, however, were quite limited—in part because sources had usually discarded the data before the committee's analysis began (some five months after the attacks) and in part because of inherent limitations in the data that were collected and retained.

The ability to report comprehensive details of the Internet's response during September 11, or during any crisis for that matter, is further constrained by a number of factors. One of the consequences of the Internet's fragmented and often proprietary measurement infrastructure is that data are taken piecemeal in diverse ways and stored in various formats. As a result, information that was available to the committee generally permitted only rough comparison with a normal or typical day in the context of a particular set of data. Measurement difficulties also arise from the size, complexity, and diversity of the Internet and from the fact that a great deal of the data that do exist are considered proprietary by the companies that collect them.

In the course of the committee's work, it became clear that a number of questions could not be answered with the available information. These included:

• *How did Internet traffic vary from normal activity during and after the attacks?* Some traffic data were available from individual ISPs, but it was not always clear how to extrapolate from these localized observations to a more generalized view.

• *What was the mix of applications used before, during, and after the attacks?* Again, some local data were available from some ISPs, but it was unclear, as above, if they constituted a collective picture.

• *How much demand was there on news services before, during, and after the attacks?* Some news services were so overwhelmed by demand that their monitoring systems shut down.

• *How much connectivity was lost as a result of the attacks? How many users were affected, and for how long? How quickly was connectivity restored?* Answering these questions would require data from a large number of ISPs or from a carefully targeted sample of ISPs.

These unanswered questions suggest that a more robust assessment of crisis events in the future will require new approaches to gathering network measurement data. In addressing how measurement of the Internet may be improved, this chapter discusses methods and tools for measurement; the data available from September 11; types of measurements required to fully assess the Internet under crisis; challenges to be faced in gathering and analyzing these measurements; and suggestions for the future.

NETWORK MEASUREMENT METHODS AND TOOLS

Since the Internet's inception, measurement has been a significant element of networking research, starting with the Network Measurement

Center at the University of California, Los Angeles, in 1970. Early on, when the system was operated as a government-funded research network, measurement was simpler owing to the explicit research character, relatively modest scale, and simple topology of the network, and to the absence of proprietary constraints. With commercialization and sustained rapid growth, the network has become much larger and more complex—making comprehensive measurement harder and more expensive—and a host of commercial interests have further limited how and where measurements can be made and who can make them. At the same time, measurement remains an important activity, particularly from the perspective of network operations.

These constraints notwithstanding, the continued interest in measuring a wide range of Internet characteristics both for operation and research has led to the development of an array of tools (though researchers' access to them has not been unfettered).

Active Measurement Tools

Active measurement tools are based on the concept of sending probe packets into the network and measuring their behavior as they flow through it. The probe packets are typically emitted from a general-purpose end-host such as a personal computer. Probe packets are sent toward a destination host by providing a target IP address (or domain name) to the measurement tool. The injection of probe packets into the network provides an indication of the routing behavior, propagation delay, queuing delay, and loss that would be experienced by normal data packets. When (and if) the probes arrive at a destination, either their arrival is logged or response packets are returned to the sender. When a response packet is returned, its arrival back at the original sender is logged, constituting the conclusion of one measurement. Active probing can also be done by approximating the behavior of typical applications, such as sending a request for a Web page.

Active probes are important because one can gain crucial insight into network conditions for a specific end-to-end path at a specific time, which may not be possible if one monitoring occurs at only a single point. Furthermore, active measurements generally do not require special participation by intermediate nodes, making them easy to deploy and execute.

While active probe tools provide important data about specific end-to-end conditions, there are a number of drawbacks to their use. First, the act of placing a probe into the network causes a perturbation (dubbed the "Heisenberg effect" by analogy to the uncertainty principle in physics) that may lead to a change in the network's operating conditions. Because of this problem, common practice is to use active measurement tools to sample the network at sufficiently low rates so as not to significantly perturb the network—avoiding, for example, significant additions to congestion. However, the resultant measurement data are limited in their ability to capture events at time scales finer than the sampling rate and are constrained by the necessarily small number of source and receiver locations. A second drawback is that any one system used to conduct active measurements is limited by routing protocols and Internet topology to measuring only a portion of the Internet. Finally, active measurement tools are limited in their ability to assess aspects of volume (for example, the total amount of traffic flowing along a given path). Some of these limitations of active probes can be addressed by passive measurement tools.

Passive Measurement Tools

Passive measurement methods are based on logging different aspects of traffic observed at specific vantage points in the network. The data that can be collected by passive means may have a variety of forms, from access logs to packet traces to detailed activity counters on routers. These data can be collected either at end-hosts or at nodes within the network. Passively collected data can be displayed in real time (as is often done by network operators) or placed in a repository for offline analysis.

Passive measurement data can provide great insight into the activities on a link or at a node. However, they have some significant drawbacks. Such data are almost always considered proprietary and are rarely made available for general analysis. Passive collection of network data can result in extremely large data sets, which greatly complicate archiving and analysis. Passive measurement tools are also prone to various types of errors that require careful attention. The subsections below describe several common passive measurement tools.

Web Access Logs

Logging access activity is a standard feature in Web server software that is usually enabled by content providers. Log entries contain the time at which a particular Web file was requested, the IP address of the requester, the name and size of the requested file, and the status code returned to the requester. Content access logs can be used to assess many aspects of server behavior, including load, content being requested, and the sources of requests.

Packet-Trace Collection

Packet traces can be a summarization of traffic (IP flow measurements) or the details of individual packets on a given link. Such measurements require access to a network device (such as a router, switch, or link splitter) or access to a broadcast local area network. A standard tool for logging individual packets is "tcpdump,"[1] which uses packet filters to capture selected packet activity from the network interface. A typical log entry from tcpdump consists of a time stamp, the source/destination IP/port numbers, the transport protocol name, details from the packet header, and details of the packet payload. Collection of this information, especially the packet payload itself, provides valuable insights into network use. However, almost all organizations that collect such detailed traces are unwilling or unable to share the traces with other parties, owing to privacy and confidentiality concerns.

Border Gateway Protocol

Because of the Internet's distributed and very dynamic operation, the individual ISPs must continuously keep each other informed about their own network's reachability. The protocol that they use for this purpose is called the Border Gateway Protocol (BGP). By examining changes in the routing information provided by BGP, one can trace changes in the status of the Internet. Each commercial ISP (e.g., UUNET or ATT) or network of a major organization (e.g., the National Science Foundation or the Massachusetts Institute of Technology) uses BGP to inform all other ISPs and network operators that it provides connectivity for particular sets of addresses and that packets destined for those addresses should be sent to it.

Such advertising of connectivity is called a BGP route announcement. Thus, ISPs adjacent to UUNET would repeat UUNET's route advertisement to their neighbors, with the added information that the relaying ISP had connectivity and thus could relay packets through to UUNET, if needed. If a neighbor's connectivity to UUNET failed for some reason, then it needs to tell its own neighbors that it can no longer relay packets through to UUNET; this information is advertised using a BGP route withdrawal. BGP update messages are logged for public use at a number of "looking glass" sites, such as Route Views.[2]

The size of a BGP routing table, which indicates how many announced paths are available, gives an overview of network status. As of June 2002,

---

[1]Tcpdump. Online at <www.tcpdump.org>.

[2]Route Views, University of Oregon. Online at <http://www.antc.uoregon.edu/routeviews>.

a typical core BGP table contained roughly 100,000 entries (the exact size depends on the vantage point). A significant drop in the size of a core routing table is an indication of some sort of connectivity loss. Observing the route advertisements and withdrawals also provides information on the Internet's health. If a route is withdrawn for an extended period of time, one may assume that some form of network outage has taken place. This failure may result from infrastructural damage, misconfiguration by an ISP, or simply scheduled maintenance. The withdrawal of all routes to a particular part of the network indicates a significant loss of connectivity. Routes that are repeatedly withdrawn and announced are an indication either of unstable links or instability in the routing system itself.

BGP tables are constructed and updated through exchanges among peer networks. However, each table only provides information on the network as seen from a given vantage point. A drop in connectivity seen at that point might, therefore, represent a local failure rather than something more widespread. Assessing the overall status of the network thus requires examining many, carefully selected BGP tables that in aggregate reflect the shape of the entire network.[3]

Simple Network Management Protocol

The Simple Network Management Protocol (SNMP) [4] is an important component in the daily operation of large-scale networks. It is the protocol used by network management systems to communicate with network elements such as routers and switches. SNMP enables network management systems both to query network elements for data and to send data to network elements. Data that are maintained and available from network elements through the SNMP are specified by a Management Information Base (MIB). This data set is gathered passively by network elements. Most of the items in the MIB data set are simple activity counters, such as the number of packets transferred on a specific link. One of the main uses of SNMP MIB data is to ensure that a network is performing within acceptable operational limits. Management systems are configured to provide multiple "views" into the network based on its topological configuration, enabling network managers to assess in nearly real time the state of their systems.

SNMP MIB data are ubiquitous in a network and could be very useful

---

[3]Q. Chen, H. Chang, R. Govindan, S. Jamin, S. Shenker, and W. Willinger. 2002. "The Origin of Power Laws in Internet Topologies Revisited," in *Proceedings of IEEE Infocom 2002,* June. New York, N.Y.

[4]W. Stevens. 1994. *TCP/IP Illustrated, Vol. 1: The Protocols.* Addison-Wesley, Boston.

in assessing the state of the Internet during a crisis. However, they are typically considered proprietary and are only available to the operators running a specific network.

MEASUREMENT CHALLENGES

Proprietary Data

As indicated above, business and legal considerations can mean that most data about Internet behavior during crisis conditions may never be made public. If these data were available, the assessment of Internet behavior during a crisis, or indeed, at any other time, would be greatly simplified. There would be challenges in organizing and normalizing the data, but these procedures would readily lend themselves to scientific methods. However, convincing large network providers to make their data publicly available is at best an uphill battle and at worst a pipe dream. An alternative approach would be to mandate reporting by ISPs to an agency such as the Federal Communications Commission (indeed, reports of certain types of outages in the public telephone network must be so filed under present rules).

Consistency in Data and Analysis

There is no guarantee that data gathered at different sites are consistent. Time stamps, units, and field descriptions for data can all be different. Owing to sampling and the possibility of measurement errors, there are also issues of the basic accuracy of particular measurements. Furthermore, even if the data are consistent, the tools and data analysis methods must also be consistent in order to evaluate and validate results.

Representativeness

The heterogeneity of the Internet infrastructure and its users, applications, protocols, and media all render it difficult if not impossible to make representative statements about overall Internet behavior on the basis of a small number of measurements. This heterogeneity manifests itself in several ways, such as:

- *Available bandwidth.* Wireless users with a low-bandwidth connection to the Internet exhibit dramatically different behavior from users with corporate high-bandwidth connections. High-bandwidth users are much more likely to access multimedia content such as video streams.
- *Network congestion.* The levels of congestion in the Internet vary

dramatically. Many parts of the United States have high-bandwidth links with relatively low utilization. In contrast, other parts of the network have modest capacity and high utilization, which in turn result in high loss rates for packets traversing them.

• *Connectivity.* Some parts of the network are richly connected with many alternate paths, while other parts of the Internet are dependent on only a single link for connectivity.

Such factors make it virtually impossible to assess the health of the Internet without measurement data from a large and diverse set of vantage points.

THE FUTURE: TARGETED ASSESSMENT DURING A CRISIS

This section discusses what data would be required for a more robust assessment of Internet characteristics during crisis events (or any other time) and how these data might be gathered.

Global Network Monitoring

A thorough analysis of Internet behavior during crisis events requires clean, consistent data from a number of vantage points across all network layers. In a general sense, this means that the following data are required from sufficient numbers and types of protocols, networks, geographic points, and time scales:

• Application and service-level data such as Web server logs,
• End-to-end connectivity, delay, and loss data such as those gathered by active probes,
• Packet traffic data such as IP flow or router Management Information Base logs, and
• Global interdomain routing data.

Only modest quantities of data from each category in this list were available for September 11. Better understanding of future events will depend on the consistency, perspective (geographic and topological location), and time scale of measurement data.

Perhaps the most extreme means for gathering data robustly during a crisis would be to construct a measurement infrastructure targeted for this specific purpose. But a more practical approach would be the creation of a well-defined data repository into which network operators could submit data collected throughout the event. This approach would have the significant benefit of not requiring the facilitator of the repository to deploy and manage measurement systems. It might also enable data gathering from areas of the Internet that would otherwise be inaccessible. The drawbacks of this approach would be the difficulties associated with maintaining consistency in submitted data and relying on others to choose where the data are gathered. It would also require the establishment of well-defined policies on submission, privacy, and the use of data. Another challenge would be in calibrating methods of analysis for comparing or aggregating different data sources.

Maintaining a robust set of network data would also provide a firmer basis for simulating Internet behavior. Models could be used to assess how the Internet might perform in different failure modes. This capability could provide key insights into Internet vulnerabilities and potentially alleviate circumstances in which connectivity was lost, as occurred in several instances on September 11.

Targeted Measurement During a Crisis

Effective assessment of Internet behavior during a crisis would be greatly enhanced by the ability to adjust the scope of what is being measured in accordance with the specific situation. This kind of targeted assessment would be facilitated by the establishment of a general repository of contact information for network operators, content providers, and groups that run network-monitoring infrastructures. Two examples of such lists are Jared Mauch's compilation of information on network operations[5] and CAIDA's compilation of Internet measurement activities.[6] When a crisis arises, measurement data could quickly be solicited from groups on this list in areas that are topologically close (from an Internet perspective) to the geographic location of the crisis. Maintaining such a repository would require resources; however, restricting the objective to targeted measurement of medium to large-scale events would make this effort much more manageable. Making sense of measurements taken during particular network events also requires the capture of a baseline "normal day."[7]

---

[5]See <http://puck.nether.net/netops>.

[6]See <http://www.caida.org/analysis/performance/measinfra>.

[7]The characterization of a typical Internet day is discussed in more detail in Computer Science and Telecommunications Board, National Research Council, 2001, *Looking Over the Fence at Networks: A Neighbor's View of Networking Research*, National Academy Press, Washington, D.C.

Appendixes

Appendix A

Participants in March 5-6, 2002, Workshop

Fred Baker, Cisco
Aristotle Balogh, Verisign
Paul Barford, University of Wisconsin, Madison
K. Claffy, Cooperative Association for Internet Data Analysis
David D. Clark, Massachusetts Institute of Technology
Chase Cotton, Sprint Technology Services
Sean Donelan, SBC Communications
Stuart I. Feldman, IBM Research
Geoffrey S. French, Veridian
Deirdre Kostick, AT&T
Timothy Lance, NYSERNet
William LeFebvre, CNN Internet Technologies
Geraldine MacDonald, America Online
Bruce Maggs, Akamai/Carnegie Mellon
David Moore, Cooperative Association for Internet Data Analysis
Andrew T. Ogielski, Renesys
Craig Partridge, BBN Technologies
Vern Paxson, International Computer Science Institute's Center for
    Internet Research
John S. Quarterman, Matrix NetSystems
Lee Rainie, Pew Internet and American Life
Jennifer Rexford, AT&T Labs–Research
David Safford, IBM Research
Steve Schneider, State University of New York, Institute of Technology
Anthony Townsend, New York University
Mary K. Vernon, University of Wisconsin, Madison

Appendix B

Committee Member and Staff Biographies

Craig Partridge, *Chair,* is a chief scientist at BBN Technologies (a Verizon company), where he leads a variety of Internet-related research efforts. His current major projects involve an innovative way to trace Internet packets to their origin and the use of signal processing techniques to perform traffic analysis. In the mid-1980s, Dr. Partridge designed the process by which Internet e-mail is routed. He is the chairman of the Association for Computing Machinery's Special Interest Group in Data Communication (one of the two major professional societies in data communications). He is the former editor-in-chief of ACM's *Computer Communication Review* and of the *IEEE Network Magazine,* and a consulting editor for Addison-Wesley's Professional Computing series. A member of the technical advisory boards of Matrix.Net and Arbor Networks, Dr. Partridge is a former consulting professor at Stanford University and he spent 1990 as a visiting research fellow at the Swedish Institute of Computer Science. He is a fellow of the Institute of Electrical and Electronics Engineers (IEEE) and holds A.B., M.Sc., and Ph.D. degrees from Harvard University. Dr. Partridge was a member of the Computer Science and Telecommunications Board (CSTB) committee that authored *The Internet's Coming of Age,* and he is also a member of CSTB's Committee on Internet Navigation and the Domain Name System.

Paul Barford is an assistant professor of computer science at the University of Wisconsin, Madison. His research interests include wide area networks and protocols, Internet measurement, network performance

74

modeling and analysis, and the World Wide Web. Dr. Barford is on the Technical Advisory Board of epicRealm, Inc., and serves on the program committees of ACM SIGMETRICS 2003, the IEEE Workshop on Internet Applications 2003, the 2002 Institute for Pure and Applied Mathematics (IPAM) Workshop on Large Scale Communications Networks, and the 2002 International Performance and Dependability Symposium. Dr. Barford is the leader of the Badger Internet Group (BIG), which conducts research in network performance and network management. He received his Ph.D. in computer science from Boston University in December 2000.

David D. Clark graduated from Swarthmore College in 1966 and received his Ph.D. from the Massachusetts Institute of Technology (MIT) in 1973. He has worked since then at the MIT Laboratory for Computer Science, where he is currently a senior research scientist in charge of the Advanced Network Architecture Group. Dr. Clark's research interests include networks, network protocols, operating systems, distributed systems, and computer and communications security. After receiving his Ph.D., he worked on the early stages of the ARPANET and on the development of token-ring local-area-network technology. Since the mid-1970s, Dr. Clark has been involved in the development of the Internet. From 1981 to 1989, he acted as its chief protocol architect and chaired the Internet Activities Board. His current research area is protocols and architectures for very large and very high speed networks. Specific activities include extensions to the Internet to support real-time traffic, explicit allocation of service, pricing, and new network technologies. In the security area, Dr. Clark participated in the early development of the multilevel secure Multics operating system. He developed an information security model that stresses integrity of data rather than disclosure control. Dr. Clark is a fellow of the ACM and the IEEE and is a member of the National Academy of Engineering. He received the ACM Special Interest Group in Data Communication (SIGCOMM) award and the IEEE award in International Communications, as well as the IEEE Hamming Award for his work on the Internet. He is a consultant to a number of companies and serves on several technical advisory boards. Dr. Clark chaired the committee that produced the CSTB report *Computers at Risk: Safe Computing in the Information Age*. He also served on the committees that produced the CSTB reports *Toward a National Research Network*; *Realizing the Information Future: The Internet and Beyond*; and *The Unpredictable Certainty: Information Infrastructure Through 2000*. He currently chairs the Computer Science and Telecommunications Board of the National Academies.

Sean Donelan is director-Internet security at SBC Communications. He has extensive experience with peering, fiber-optic cable cuts, data center security, cracking, power outages, and other networking topics. Before joining SBC, Mr. Donelan was design engineer at Equinix, where he was responsible for the technical standards of Equinix Internet Business Exchange centers and identifying new technologies. Before joining Equinix, he was a principal technical staff member at AT&T Laboratories. There he worked on Internet service for Concert, the joint venture between AT&T and British Telecommunications. He also acted as the lead Internet service provider (ISP) representative to the U.S. Year 2000 Coordination Center for ISPs that were not represented by first-tier providers. Prior to joining AT&T, Mr. Donelan was at Data Research Associates (DRA) for 14 years. He served in a variety of positions, from database programmer to senior network architect. He was responsible for building a nationwide backbone network that provides Internet and database services to more than 3,000 libraries. At DRA, Mr. Donelan wrote the first commercial library catalog search engine on the World Wide Web.

Vern Paxson received his M.S. and Ph.D. degrees from the University of California, Berkeley. He is a senior scientist at the International Computer Science Institute's Center for Internet Research in Berkeley and a staff computer scientist at the Lawrence Berkeley National Laboratory, and he serves on the technical advisory boards of a number of Internet-related companies. Dr. Paxson's research focuses on Internet measurement and on detection and analysis of Internet attacks. His doctoral thesis, which pioneered the use of "measurement infrastructure" for conducting large-scale Internet measurement studies, was awarded the Sakrison Memorial Prize of the University of California, Berkeley, for outstanding dissertation research; this work was also cited as best student paper from ACM SIGCOMM for a paper derived from one of its chapters. Dr. Paxson's study of Internet routing was awarded the IEEE Communications Society's William R. Bennett Prize Paper Award, and he was again awarded the Bennett Prize for his paper (with S. Floyd) "Difficulties in Simulating the Internet" in *IEEE/ACM Transactions on Networking*. His work on the "Bro" intrusion detection system was awarded best paper at the USENIX Security Symposium, and subsequent research on detecting backdoors led to a USENIX Security Symposium best student paper award for his student coauthor (Y. Zhang). Dr. Paxson serves on the editorial board of *IEEE/ACM Transactions on Networking*. He has been active in the Internet Engineering Task Force (<www.ietf.org>), chairing working groups on performance metrics, Transport Control Protocol (TCP) implementation, and endpoint-congestion management, and he has served on the Internet Engineering Steering Group as an area director for transport. Dr. Paxson has coauthored 10 requests for comments (RFCs) specifying Internet Engineering Task Force standards and practices. As current chair of the Internet Research Task Force (<www.irtf.org>), he is an ex officio member of the Internet Architecture Board (<www.iab.org>). Dr. Paxson served as program committee co-chair for the 2002 ACM SIGCOMM conference, and he is program committee chair for the 2003 USENIX Security Symposium. He was a founding member (in 2001) of the Internet Measurement Workshop, and continues to serve on its steering committee. Paxson was a member of the committee that produced CSTB's *Looking Over the Fence at Networks: A Neighbor's View of Networking Research.*

Jennifer Rexford is a member of the network management and performance department at AT&T Labs–Research in Florham Park, New Jersey. Her research focuses on routing protocols and traffic measurement, with the goal of developing new methods and tools for operating large Internet Protocol networks. Dr. Rexford serves on the steering committee for the Internet Measurement Workshop, the editorial board of *IEEE/ACM Transactions on Networking*, and the advisory boards of ACM SIGCOMM, Arbor Networks, and MentorNet. She is a senior member of the IEEE and co-author of the book *Web Protocols and Practice: HTTP/1.1, Networking Protocols, Caching, and Traffic Measurement* (Addison-Wesley, 2001) with Balachander Krishnamurthy. Dr. Rexford received her B.S.E. degree in electrical engineering from Princeton University in 1991, and her M.S.E. and Ph.D. degrees in computer science and electrical engineering from the University of Michigan in 1993 and 1996, respectively.

Mary K. Vernon is a professor and Vilas Associate both in the computer sciences department and industrial engineering department at the University of Wisconsin, Madison. Her research targets the development and state-of-the-art application of computer systems performance modeling techniques that can be used to design new near-optimal computer/communication system architectures with known performance properties. Dr. Vernon has made contributions to commercial bus arbiters, cache coherence protocols, mesh interconnection networks with wormhole routing, the Sequent Symmetry bus design, commercial memory system design methods, analysis of parallel shared memory system architectures with complex modern processors, the Cray UNICOS operating system semaphore architecture, production parallel system job scheduling policies, the design of large parallel and distributed applications, scalable protocols for on-demand streaming with packet loss recovery, optimized media content delivery networks, media content delivery cost models, customized mean value analysis modeling techniques, LogP modeling techniques, task graph analysis techniques, interpolation approximation techniques, and Petri net modeling techniques. Her current research includes development of analytic modeling methods, networked systems security, scalable multimedia delivery protocols and content distribution networks, design of widely distributed adaptive applications, and job scheduling policies for the TeraGrid. Dr. Vernon received the National Science Foundation (NSF) Presidential Young Investigator Award in 1985, the NSF Faculty Award for Women in Science and Engineering in 1990, the ACM Fellow Award in 1995 for "fundamental contributions to performance analysis of parallel computer architectures and for leadership in the computing research community," and a University of Wisconsin, Madison Vilas Associate Award in 2000. She is a co-inventor on two U.S. patents for bus arbitration protocols and on four recent U.S. patent applications for new streaming media delivery protocols. She has published more than 80 technical papers, including three that have won best-paper awards. She has served on the editorial boards of *IEEE Transactions on Parallel and Distributed Systems* and *IEEE Transactions on Software Engineering*, the 1993 NSF Blue Ribbon Panel for High Performance Computing, the NSF Computer Information Science and Engineering Advisory Board, the board of directors of the Computing Research Association, external advisory committees for various engineering colleges and computer science departments, and as recent chair of the ACM SIGMETRICS.

Staff

Jon Eisenberg, *Study Director*, is a senior program officer with the Computer Science and Telecommunications Board (CSTB) of the National Academies. At CSTB, he has been study director for a diverse body of work, including a series of studies exploring networking technologies and Internet and broadband policy. Current studies include an examination of emerging wireless technologies and spectrum policy and a review of the National Archives and Records Administration's digital materials preservation strategy. In 1995-1997 he was a AAAS Science, Engineering, and Diplomacy Fellow at the U.S. Agency for International Development where he worked on environmental management, technology transfer, and telecommunications policy issues. He received his Ph.D. in physics from the University of Washington in 1996 and a B.S. in physics with honors from the University of Massachusetts at Amherst in 1988.

As its Director, **Marjory Blumenthal** manages the Computer Science and Telecommunications Board of the National Academies—a 20-member Board of leaders from industry and academia—and its many expert project committees and staff. She designs, develops, directs, and oversees collaborative study projects, workshops, and symposia on technical, strategic, and policy issues in computing and telecommunications. These activities address trends in the relevant science and technology, their uses, and economic and social impacts, providing independent and authoritative analysis and/or a neutral meeting ground for senior people in government, industry, and academia. Marjory is the principal author and/or substantive editor of numerous reports and articles. The majority of her work has been interdisciplinary. Before joining CSTB, Marjory was manager, Competitive Analysis and Planning, for GE Information Services. There she directed an analytical team supporting business development, product marketing, and field sales and developed business alliances for domestic and international network services. Previously she was a project director at the former Office of Technology Assessment, evaluating computer and communications technology trends and their social and economic impacts. There, among other things, she produced an internationally acclaimed study of computers in manufacturing and their implications for industries and employment. Marjory is a member of the Santa Fe Institute Science Board, the Advisory Board of the Pew Internet & American Life Project, the TPRC Board of Directors, the editorial board of ACM Transactions on Internet Technology, and the ACM, AEA, and IEEE. In 1998 Marjory was a visiting scientist at the Massachusetts Institute of Technology, Laboratory for Computer Science. At MIT she developed and taught a course on public policy for computer science graduate students and pursued personal research interests. Marjory did her undergraduate work at Brown University and her graduate work (as an NSF graduate fellow) at Harvard University.

David Padgham, research associate, began with CSTB in 1998, working on, among other things, the studies that produced *Trust in Cyberspace, Funding a Revolution*, and *Realizing the Potential of C4I*. More recently, he has assisted with the research and production of *Broadband: Bringing Home the Bits, LC21: A Digital Strategy for the Library of Congress, The Internet's Coming of Age, Looking Over the Fence at Networks*, and *Information Technology Research, Innovation, and E-Government*. Currently, he is providing research support for two CSTB projects: one focusing on privacy in the information age and one looking at digital archiving and the National Archives and Records Administration. He holds a master's degree in library and information science (2001) from the Catholic University of America in Washington, D.C., as well as a bachelor of arts degree (1996) in English from Warren Wilson College in Asheville, N.C.

Kristen Batch is a research associate with the Computer Science and Telecommunications Board. She will be involved with upcoming projects focusing on wireless communication technologies and telecommunications research and development. While pursuing an M.A. in International Communications from American University, she interned at the National

Telecommunications and Information Administration, in the Office of International Affairs, and at the Center for Strategic and International Studies, in the Technology and Public Policy Program. She also earned a B.A. from Carnegie Mellon University in literary and cultural studies and in Spanish, and she received two travel grants to conduct independent research in Spain.

D.C. Drake joined the staff of CSTB in September 1999. He is currently handling work on a number of projects, including one on critical information infrastructure protection and the law and another on a research agenda for counterterrorism. He came to Washington, D.C., in January 1999 after finishing a master's in international politics and communications at the University of Kentucky and earning a B.A. in international relations and German from Rhodes College in 1996. He has worked for the Hanns-Seidl Foundation in Munich, Germany, and in Washington, D.C., for the National Conference of State Legislatures' International Programs Office and for the Majority Staff of the Senate Foreign Relations Committee.

Janet Briscoe is the administrative officer for the Computer Science and Telecommunications Board. She has been a part of the team since 1997. Janet has over 15 years of experience in administrative management. Her areas of expertise include process improvement, problem solving, problem resolution, troubleshooting, time management, and organizational effectiveness. Prior to joining CSTB, Janet worked as a support services manager for Norrell Corporation (1991-1996), where she was contracted to provide administrative management services to two of Norrell Corporation's clients (Ernst & Young and IBM). She also worked as a word-processing manager for Shannon & Luchs (1986-1991). Janet is very active in her local church and community, where she serves in several leadership positions. She is also a volunteer for Junior Achievement of the Washington, D.C., area. Janet holds a B.S. degree in organizational management from Columbia Union College.